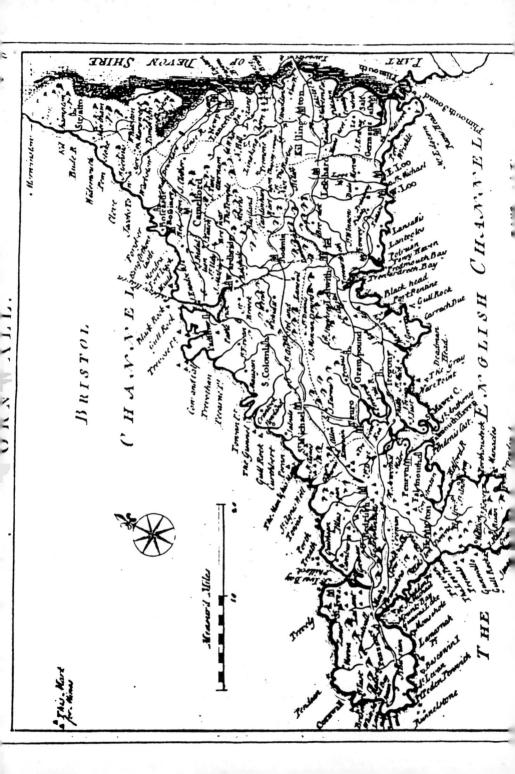

CORNWALL FROM THE NEWSPAPERS: 1781-93

BY DR.JAMES WHETTER

Lyfrow

Trelyspen

First published in 2000 by Lyfrow Trelyspen, The Roseland Institute, Gorran

Copyright © 2000 Dr.James Whetter

British Library Cataloguing in Publication Data.
A catalogue record of this book is available from the British Library.

ISBN 0 9514510 8 1

Designed and printed by Lyfrow Trelyspen and Palace Printers, Lostwithiel.

The cover is a reproduction of an engraving of 1795 of Polston bridge over the Tamar with Launceston castle and church in the background.

PREFACE

Looking around for topics for the magazine I edit, the Cornish Banner/An Baner Kernewek, in the early 1980s I thought an interesting feature could be made with extracts from the main newspaper that circulated in Cornwall in the late 18th century, the Sherborne Mercury. So over the following 12 years I produced a selection of references relating to Cornwall - the paper also covered other south western counties. More recently I wrote for the magazine a series of short biographies of Cornish people who lived in that century and did intend to include a resumé of the material from the paper as one article. However, as often seems the case, the work ended up too long and I had to exclude it. Having got assistance in the past winter with my publishing activities it occurred to me to produce it as a separate work, illustrated with contemporary prints, a taster for the main one to be published later in the year. So here it is and I hope people will enjoy it and gain some knowledge and feel of the period from it.

My thanks to people who have assisted, Verena Vollertsen for keying in the material and helping with lay-out and illustrations, the librarians at the Local History Studies Library, Redruth where I consulted the microfilm of the Sherborne Mercury for the feature for the Cornish Banner, Angela Broome at the Royal Institution, Truro, librarians at the Public Library there, Peter Brierley for photographing engravings of the period and the staffs of Palace Printers and Larkbeare Binding Services in Devon for their help with the later stages of the production.

The Roseland Institute, Gorran 7th June 2000

rak Ern ha Laureen

CONTENTS

PREFACE   v

FARMS   1
"SHEWS" & "SURVEYS"; HORSES   2
DOGS; AGRICULTURAL IMPROVEMENT   3
GARDENS AND FRUIT TREES; WOODLANDS   4
MILLS; MINES   6
FISHING   8
OTHER TRADES AND CRAFTS   9
PUBLIC HOUSES   11
SHIPPING   15
SHIPWRECKS   16
SMUGGLING   18
INLAND TRANSPORT   20
BRIDGES AND PAVEMENTS   22
NEW HOUSES   23
SERVANTS   24
WORKHOUSES   25
RUNAWAYS   26
SCHOOLS   30
ANNUITANT SOCIETIES   33
THE CHURCH   34
ECCLESIASTICAL COURTS   35
DEBTS OWING; MARITAL PROBLEMS   36
DEFAMATION OF CHARACTER   38
VANDALISM   40
ASSIZES   41
ELECTIONS   46
LOST AND STOLEN   47
PILLS AND MEDICINES   54
DOCTORS; HOSPITAL   56
LIBRARY; BOOKS   57
MUSIC AND THE THEATRE; CLUBS   58
SPORTS   59
FAIRS; CELEBRATIONS   62
NEWS ITEMS: TRAGEDIES AND MIRACULOUS ESCAPES   64
FIRES; UNUSUAL CRIMES   66
DEATHS   67
MARRIAGES; BIRTHS   68
METEOR AND EARTHQUAKE; ANTI-SLAVERY; LOYAL ADDRESSES   70

ILLUSTRATIONS

FRONT COVER POLSTON BRIDGE 1795

BACK COVER VIGNETTE FROM BRITTON AND BRAYLEY, 1802

FRONTISPIECE...CONTEMPORARY MAP OF CORNWALL

1. LAUNCESTON CASTLE 1784   5

2. TREMATON CASTLE 1787   13

3. ST.GERMANS PRIORY 1787   21

4. RESTORMEL CASTLE 1784   29

5. FOWEY HAVEN AND CASTLES 1786   37

6. PROBUS CHURCH FROM BRITTON AND BRAYLEY, 1802   45

7. TEHIDY PARK 1781   53

8. PENGERSICK CASTLE 1786   61

9. ST.MICHAELS MOUNT 1786   69

CORNWALL FROM THE NEWSPAPERS: EXTRACTS FROM THE SHERBORNE MERCURY 1781-93

FARMS

Much of the material in the Sherborne Mercury in this period consists of advertisements and legal notices. Naturally farming and sales and letting of land are a major feature. Lacking much social and human interest just a few examples may suffice. Big holdings were usually let for 7, 14 or 21 years. The quality of the land, closeness of markets and sources of manure were important factors in determining their value. On 20th December 1781 Messrs. Rawle and Harvey, attornies at Liskeard advertised "the capital barton or farm of Golden, Probus. Good dwelling house, large barns, stables and other convenient buildings. Upwards of 500 acres of good arable, meadow and pasture land. 1½ miles from Grampound and Tregony, 6 from Truro, Penryn and Falmouth." Smaller was the tenement of Penpoll in Phillack which was to be let for 14 years in May 1791. It consisted of "130 acres of arable and pasture ground, 15 acres of crofts and moors, a dwelling house, barn, stable and other out-houses, all in good repair, and situated near the river of Hayle, where sea sand and other good manure may be conveniently had; distant from Penzance eight miles, Marazion five, and St.Ives four miles, and in a mining country, where a farmer cannot fail in making the best advantage of the produce of said tenement".

The traditional lease for properties was for 99 years or for as long as three named lives lived. Its use was declining in this period though it was still employed for some smaller tenements. "A public survey at the house of Samuel Pentecost in St.Austell on Friday 13th September 1782 for selling the lease for three lives to be named by purchaser of tenements of Polrudden and Mannells near Pentewan, consisting of 45 acres of land, well watered, pleasantly situated and very near sea sand, which is most excellent manure. The dwelling house and outhouses are slated and may easily be made a commodious and genteel residence". Among property advertised for sale was "that capital and desirable Estate, Mansion-House, and Premises, called Lunna, in the parish of St.Neot" on 20th May 1790. It consisted of "a large, handsome, modern built dwelling house, which at a small expence may be rendered fit for the reception of a genteel family; very complete barn, stables, and outhouses, a walled garden, good kitchen garden, 6 acres of orchards, well stocked with young fruit-trees, in excellent condition, and about 60 acres of rich arable and pasture land, in a good state of cultivation. Lunna lies in a very pleasant situation, about six miles from the several market-towns of Bodmin, Lostwithiel, and Liskeard, and is in every respect well adapted for the residence either of a gentleman or a respectable farmer". As in the last instance there was an overlap between farming enterprises and property which might appeal to gentlemen whose concern was less with agriculture than with having a residence which would be improved by having a small estate attached to it.

"SHEWS" & "SURVEYS"

Farmers sold their livestock and other produce at markets and fairs. In February 1788 it was announced that there was to be a "shew of cattle" on the Tuesdays after Ladyday and Michaelmas at Grampound that was "to be free of all tolls for three years. N.B. Gentlemen are already acquainted with the large assortment of cattle shewn on the established fair days, January 18 and June 11". A sale of cattle was held at Perranwell in Perranarworthal on 10th May 1792 and the first Thursday in September. "There will be a continuance annually, without any alteration in future of the preferred days for holding the said sales." Public "surveys" or auctions were held at the deaths of farmers, when they retired or otherwise gave up business. A public survey was held at Bake in St.Germans on 2nd May 1793 of "all the valuable Stock and Implements of Husbandry on the said Farm; consisting of 12 oxen; 4 steers fit for the yoke; 1 bull, one year and half old; 9 cows and calves; 6 cows, now with calf; 13 two year old bullocks; 17 yearlings; 3 rearing calves; 7 good saddle, cart, and labour horses; 2 mares with foal; 2 colts; 80 ewes and lambs; 75 one year old sheep; 13 large pigs; 2 sows and farrows".

HORSES

Horses, which played such an important part in farm work, transport and communications, were naturally much valued and periodically were advertised for sale. In January 1785 there was offered "A very handsome, strong, good horse, fifteen hands high, nine years old, used to draw in a single horse chaise, warranted sound in every respect, very fit for a hackney, post-chaise, or diligence. For particulars apply to Mr. Coode, at Penryn". Stallions were in demand for serving mares. In the same month "Saint Germans will cover this season at Seveock, near Truro, one guinea the mare and two shillings the servant. Saint Germans was got by Old Forester (the sire of Grecian and other good runners), his dam by Blank. He was a very good runner, and since he was taken out of training, has been, and now is, a very good hunter". Chaises, "whiskeys", and other carriages were often offered with horses. "To be sold, a very handsome, good chaise, almost new, with harness complete for a pair of horses; also with or without a good pair of horses. Any person whom this may suit, may apply to John Coad, at the Duke's Head Inn, Helstone. April 14, 1786".

Because they were so valued they regularly figured among the animals "stolen or strayed". "Stolen or strayed out of the fields of John Trevenen esq., of Helston, a dark sorrel mare, about 13 hands and a half or 14 hands high with a mulish tail. One guinea reward for return. There is reason to believe she was taken out of field by night by means of the unhanging the gate. Whoever will give information about the offenders, so that they may be apprehended, shall receive 5 gns. reward on their conviction. May 1783".

DOGS

Dogs were used around the farm for rounding up stock etc. Those that were lost, however, seem mainly to have been of the sporting variety, employed for shooting and hunting. "Strayed on Wednesday 29th 1783 from Catch-French, St.Germans, a spaniel bitch, about a year old; her back is black, her face, neck and feet white, her tail rather long; she is very shy and answers to the name of Flora. Whoever, will bring her to Catch French or to Mr. Hawkey, sadler, in Liskeard, or will give information where she is to be found, shall receive one guinea reward. N.B. It is supposed she strayed towards Tregony".

AGRICULTURAL IMPROVEMENT

Agricultural improvement was in the air in the period and regularly in advertisements the good features of farms which could be developed were drawn attention to. On 1st December 1792 there was formed at a meeting at the White Hart, Bodmin the Cornwall Agricultural Society. It was resolved "1st. That it is the interest of every country to promote industry and agriculture in its inhabitants. 2d. That an association be formed for promoting these objects, and that a subscription be entered into for that purpose. 3d. That a Select Committee be appointed, consisting of the seven following gentlemen, to consider of plans, and lay the same before a general meeting, to be held at Bodmin the second day of the next summer Assizes. Sir William Molesworth, Bart., Sir Francis Bassett, Bart., Rev. H. Hawkins Tremayne, Colonel Rodd, Rev. Thomas Trevenen, R.L.Gwatkin, Esq., John Thomas, Esq., Vice-Warden. 4th That the thanks of this meeting be given to Sir William Molesworth, Bart. for having called the attention of the county to so useful an undertaking." The outcome was the formation of the Royal Cornwall Agricultural Association and the holding of the Royal Cornwall Shows, whose bicentenary was celebrated in 1993.

GARDENS AND FRUIT TREES

Increasing attention was being paid to gardens and fruit trees and in the sale of houses, their possession was seen as an attraction. A wide variety of trees was offered for sale by William Mathews, nurseryman, of Truro on 10th November 1790 - "a large quantity of Elms of all sizes and sorts, from 14 feet high to 6 feet high, now all fit for planting; likewise four different sorts of Ash of the same height; Sycamore: Planes; Horse and Spanish Chestnuts; Oak; Beech; Firs of different sorts; Poplars; Walnuts; Limes &c. &c. With a large quantity of very fine Apple Trees, now all fit for planting out for orchards. All sorts of Fruit Trees for walls. Trained or Young Shrubs, Evergreens, &c. to be sold as cheap as in London or elsewhere". At Liskeard a nursery and fruit garden was to be let in December 1790 "with upwards of 10,000 apple trees, from one to ten years old from the graft, all of the best bearing kinds of table and cyder fruit, and a quantity now to graft, together with about 300 cherry trees; there is likewise in the prime of bearing about 150 apple trees of choice fruit, and 70 cherry trees, with a quantity of gooseberries, currants, strawberries &c." Further application should be made to "Mr. Matthew Gourd, the owner thereof, who means to retire from the business, which hath been carried on in the family, with great success, for upwards of 50 years". On 9th January 1792 there was offered for sale at Duloe in the heart of cider making country "on reasonable terms, on the tenement of Hill, belonging to Henry Bettenson, situate in the parish of Duloe, about 20,000 Young Apple Trees, of the best kinds for cyder, the greater part of which are now fit to be transplanted".

WOODLANDS

Before the development of metals and alloys for industrial, agricultural and domestic purposes wood was used extensively and the management of woodlands occupied farmers and others interested in their products. Oak and other trees were regularly sold and coppice woods offered. "On Saturday the 12th day of June next [1790], by three o' clock in the afternoon, a Public Survey will be held at the house of Mr. Thomas Rivers, within the borough of Truro... for selling 200 trees, viz. 98 elms, 40 ash and 62 oak, now marked, numbered, and growing on the Barton of Treworder, in the parish of Kenwyn aforesaid, about three miles from Truro river, and conveniently situate for carriage of the timber to the mines". On 6th January 1792 was advertised "To be sold, All that Coppice growing on Dunmeer Wood, in the parish of Bodmin... containing about 200 acres. The greater part of the coppice is upwards of 30 years growth. Dunmeer wood is only two miles from Slade's-Bridge, where the river, which flows into the sea at Padstow, (opposite to Ireland) is navigable. For this purpose a Sale

4

Launceston Castle, Cornwall. Pl. 1.

Published Nov.ʳ 24ᵗʰ 1784 by S. Hooper.

will be held at the Publick House, at Washaway, very near to the wood, on Saturday the 28th day of this instant January, by four o'clock in the afternoon."

MILLS

An important part in agricultural life was played by water mills at this time and when being sold or let their attractions were promoted. Two at Penryn were offered in 1786 for the remainder of the term of 99 years on three good lives or for 7, 14 or 21 years - "all those two water grist-mills, near the town quay of the borough of Penryn, lately put into complete repair, and well situated for carrying on the bag corn trade, with a convenient dwelling house and out houses adjoining the same; to be sold either separate or together with a meadow of about one acre of land near the said borough, and now held on the same three lives. For which purpose a survey will be held at the Cross Keys, in Penryn, on Monday 10th July, 1786, at 4 p.m." In January the following year the Lanherne Grist Mill was offered for 99 years on three lives to be named by the purchaser. It "hath two pair of stones, and room for three; and during summer, and the dryest season, hath always water enough for at least one pair. All the numerous tenants of the manor of Lanherne are obliged to grind all the corn and grain (to be used when ground) on each and every of their respective tenements". Windmills were not unknown and the attention of millwrights was drawn to a "survey" to be held "on 31st January 1785 at Mr. William Edward's, innkeeper, upon the islands of Scilly, for rebuilding the windmill there".

MINES

Tin and copper mining was playing a major part in the Cornish economy at this time. Shares in the enterprises were often held in small fractions like those in fishing and other industries. In 1785 the Helston attorney, Christopher Wallis, advertised "the undermentioned shares in the following very prosperous, rich, extensive and profitable mines, on which are erecting the new improved fire-engines, and the greatest hopes of success are well founded, in expectation of much gains from these adventures. Lot 1. One 32nd in Wheal Crenver in Crowan; Lot 2 Eight shares in 150 parts in Wheel Reeth in Germoe and Breage; Lot 3. One 23th in the Great Work in Breage. For which purpose surveys will be held at the Angel Inn, in Helston, on Monday 9th May 1785, at 5 o'clock precisely". On 1st December 1791 there was sold at the house of William Gribble, innkeeper, in the parish of Gwennap, "One sixteenth in Tolcarn, and One Thirtieth in Poldice, both in the parish of Gwennap. One-Eighth in Wheal Pink, in the parishes of Gwennap, and Redruth. One-Eighth in Wheal St.Aubyn, One-Sixteenth in Penticka and Bucket, and One-Sixteenth in Wheal Ilbert, all in the parish of Redruth. One-Sixteenth Part in Creegbraws and Wheal Ree, in the parish of Kenwyn... all valuable tin and copper mines. One-Sixteenth in Mexico and Peru Lead Mines, in the parish of Perranzabuloe".

Some idea of crafts and trades connected with mining can be gained from adverts such as that of August 3rd 1791 for selling at Hawksmoor Mine, in the parish of Calstock "A very good Whim compleat, Stamping Mill, the Tools and Materials belonging to the Blacksmith's Shop and Burning-House, and all sorts of Tools and Materials belonging to the said mine, all very lately new, and are now in excellent order. Together with a Quantity of Oak Timber, Deal Boards, Iron, and Tin, and Copper Ore, now at grass".

In the mid-1780s competition from copper mines in Anglesey depressed the price of the metal and in May 1785 there was a meeting at Truro to consider "the very deplorable state of the copper mines in Cornwall". Among leading adventurers attending were Lord Falmouth, J. St.Aubyn, William Lemon, William Molesworth, R.A.Daniell, H. Hawkins Tremayne and the engineers, Boulton and Watt. Matthew Boulton and John Vivian were appointed to discuss with the owners of the Welsh copper mines "to put the price of fine copper at a proper standard, and to agree upon the proportion of sales." Depression in the mines led to food riots by tinners. In 1787 another meeting expressed abhorrence at "the late attempts of several misguided miners to violate the peace and good order of society... we see with equal concern the present distressed state of the mines, and that nothing shall be wanting on our part to alleviate the real distresses of the peaceable miners, and to give them every relief in our power". In 1788 the Miners Committee asked owners of waste land to grant leases to unemployed miners to help relieve them and the following year efforts were made to control the price of corn and import some barley.

The failure of the Anglesey mines in 1791 led to better prices for tin and copper and some recovery but then the war with France upset trade. In June 1792, however, it was said in a letter from Marazion - "The tin and copper mines in this neighbourhood are in a very flourishing state, and our ores bear a fine price". There were riots again this year though and, as detailed in Dr.Rowe's history of the period, in 1793. The tinners of St.Stephens rose when one of their number was committed to Launceston goal for encouraging insurrection owing to the high price of corn. A detachment of South Devon Militia was sent to Launceston to stop them releasing him. There were also riots at Padstow and Looe in early 1793 when farmers tried to export corn. The problem then slips out of our purview to be continued in Dr.Rowe's history.

Accidents occurred from time to time in mining operations. In October 1787 "one David Bussow was killed in a copper mine, near Marazion. The person who drove the horses in the whim (axis in peritrochio) let the kibbel or barrel run against the pulley, by which means upwards of 500 pounds weight of stones were thrown into a pit more than 120 yards deep, at the bottom of which was poor Bussow, who being somewhat deaf, but imagining he heard a noise, turned up his ear, and received a blow on his temple which killed him almost instantaneously. He was about to be married a second time, his banns having been twice published in the church". Early in 1792 a "melancholy accident happened at Poldice in the parish of Gwennap. Two of the labouring miners smoking their pipes in the fire-engine house, unfortunately dropped a spark into a cask of gunpowder, which blew up the place and killed two men dead on the spot, and wounded others in a very dangerous manner". At Marazion in June "as some miners were preparing to blow up a rock, near this place, a quantity of gun-powder accedentally took fire, by which means one man was terribly burnt, and 'tis supposed cannot survive. Several others narrowly escaped death".

FISHING

The other great staple of the Cornish economy was fishing. There were regular reports of the expectations of the fishery. On 27th July 1786 from Mevagissey "Last evening there appeared a prospect of pilchards. Several seans were shot, and inclosed and brought in here about eighty hundred". From Falmouth on 26th August 1790 "Vast quantities of pilchards have been taken on this coast within a few weeks past, said to be upwards of 36,000 hogsheads. This fishery, which is a very principal support of this county, has failed for several years past, in consequence of which many concerned therein have sold their parts in the netts &c. known by the name of craft, so that the whole of this year's produce will fall into the hands of few, in comparison to the numbers usually concerned. From the very large catches of pilchards, salt has become exceedingly scarce and dear... On some parts of the coast the fishermen, it is said, have neglected to take the fish which have presented themselves, merely from want of salt to cure them." Later in the year boats were arriving in Mevagissey "to take on board fish for the Streights". In the summer of 1792 - "There are several new cellars for curing pilchards, built at Causand and Kingsand, and from the appearance on the coast there is every reason to suppose the pilchard fishery will be very successful".

In the following summer - "The pilchard fishery in Cornwall promises to be both plentiful and advatageous; from 10 to 15,000 hogsheads have been cellared, and large shoals still appear in the Northern Channel, near the land. The fish taken upon the north are remarkably large and the article being in great demand, notwithstanding the war, which by reason of the vast consumption of other provisions on the continent is deemed prejudical to the sale, the curers do not expect a good price. An offer of 36s per hogshead, it is said, has been made by some of the merchants but that is considerably less than last year".

The sale of boats and equipment was often advertised. In February 1785 there was offered for sale at Mevagissey "all their very convenient dwelling houses, wherein Capt. John Furse and Alexander Baron live. Also the weaving shop and lofts, together with large commodious cellars adjoining, for curing pilchards, with a large barking furnace, press poles, weights, bucklers, and empty casks, and about 500 bushels of foreign salt; as also three sixteenths in pilchard seans." In June 1789 a public survey was held at "the house of John Carter at Newkey, in St.Columb Minor, for selling a stop sean, tuck net, 5 boats,a large stock of salt, with every other necessary material for carrying on the pilchard fishery. The situation of Newkey is the most eligible for the pilchard fishery of any place in the said county; and any purchasers may be accomodated with convenient cellars for that purpose on reasonable terms". Boats and equipment were regularly held in shares. In August 1790 there was sold "one sixteenth part in the Pope Seyne, at Portleaven, in Sithney, near Helstone, with one-sixteenth of the tock seyne's boats, salt, and other materials belonging. The whole are exceeding good repair, have taken this season 100 hogsheds of pilchards, and is now at sea".

Of course, the occupation was not without its hazards. In May 1791 - "Thursday se'nnight a melancholy accident happened near St.Ives: A fishing boat reaching towards shore, was overtaken by a sudden gust of wind, which threw her on her side, and she immediately foundered. Out of four men therein one only was saved". Sometimes the fault was due to human frailty. Also in May 1791 - "Last Thursday a French fishing vessel, burthen about 60 tons, and 24 men, sailed from hence [Mevagissey], with a fair wind, for France, soon after which she ran on shore on the rocks near this place, owing to their making too free with our English beer. The vessel lay on the rocks a considerable time, but at length suddenly fell off into the sea; she shipped a vast quantity of water, and was obliged to be brought in here. She had on board a quantity of salt and salt mackerel, the salt is much dissolved, but the fish is preserved. The vessel is much damaged."

As well as the Cornish fishery there is evidence of involvement with that of Newfoundland. In 1789 Messrs. Hearne and Treeve, the agents for the Penryn Newfoundland Company, had built sheds and other facilities on the south side of Cape Broyle Harbour in Newfoundland. The pair had overextended themselves and gone bankrupt. As well as having to sell this interest there was offered for sale shares in seines, cellars and their equipment at Mousehole, Coverack, Portscatho, Mevagissey, Gorran Haven and Porthpean.

OTHER TRADES AND CRAFTS

The Sherborne Mercury sheds light on the numerous other trades and crafts pursued in late 18th century Cornwall. Rugmaking was carried on at Bodmin workhouse as the overseers of the poor there advertised in 1781 for a new master "a middle aged man who is acquainted with the business of a rug-maker, or any other branch of the woolen manufactory and can be well recommended". John and Andrew Vivian of Camborne advertised in May 1789 for a "person capable of conducting a woollen manufactory. None need apply without producing good recommendations for honesty, sobriety, and sufficient abilities for carrying on the business in all its branches". In the spring of 1785 William Polgrean of Penzance wanted immediately "an apprentice to a sadler and ironmonger, of very extensive business, with whom a premium is expected". Around the same time Edward Harvey of Launceston wanted a journeyman wheelwright and carpenter - "one who well understands his business, will meet with constant employ and good encouragement". In April the following year Messrs. J & M. Glencross of Liskeard wanted "a shopman of indubitable character, who understands the mercery and linen-drapery business".

In February 1787 John Carne of St.Austell wanted immediately "a young man in the grocery business as shopman; and a young woman, in the millenery, drapery and mercery line. A character from each for honesty, and every requisite necessary for acquitting themselves with propriety in said branches is required". Around the same time the poorhouse at Kenwyn offered four young people as apprentices to be bound to cordwainers and taylors and Mr. Cookworthy, druggist of Plymouth and Thomas Daniell, surgeon, of Helston advertised for apprentices in their trades. A young man, Mr. R. Rowe, teacher of mathematics in Probus "wants a place as a clerk to a merchant or attorney... writes all the modern hands with fluency and expedition, knows common arithmetic, well acquainted with accompts, and can produce ample security for any trust... N.B. The advertiser has been many years used to business, and would prefer an office where there are extensive connections."

A Penzance advertiser in September 1792 wanted immediately "a sober, steady man, as a printer and bookbinder, where constant employ and good wages will be given. Any person whom this may suit is desired to apply to Mr. William Stevens, at Penzance... N.B. As the person advertised for is to superintend the business, no one need apply who cannot be well recommended for ability and sobriety." In January 1793 a writer was "wanted immediately by T.Warren, attorney at law, Truro, who understands accounts, the general business of an attorney's office, and can be well recommended for his honesty and sobriety". House-carpenters and joiners were wanted at the same place in February 1793, "Six or eight very good hands in the above branches. Sober, steady men will meet with constant employ and every encouragement, by applying to William Wood, builder, in Truro". Hatmakers at Truro, C.Colliver, and Penryn, M.Colliver, in May 1793 "wanted two or three journeymen hatmakers; good workmen will meet with great encouragement and constant employ" while in the same advertisement a journeyman bookbinder was wanted by W.Harry of Truro. Sobriety of applicants was regularly stressed as if that were a problem in the period. With distress and disease prevalent, all the smuggled liquor, the cider made on the farms, excessive consumption of alcohol was no doubt common though it is not often referred to. The advertisements for workmen do also suggest that the economy was expanding in the period. Cornwall was in the front line of the war against France and, as so often, war conditions appear to have provided a boost for farming and industry.

Among the businesses to let and for sale in the columns of the Sherborne Mercury in the period were - a malt house in the centre of Falmouth in 1782, cellars, warehouses at the quay in Penzance in 1784 "well situated for any kind of mercantile business", a millinery business at Falmouth, a "new-built malt-house" at Millbrook the same year and a malt-house at St.Clement in 1785. In 1786 John Cock of the Polvarth Manufactory, near St.Mawes, sought custom for his business in "cordage, sail-cloth,

10

poldavies, and other canvas, netting, twine &c."; "a commodious coal quay, near Sunny Corner, and a coal yard, near the New Bridge, Truro" was to let and Moyle and Paul of Redruth advertised their mercery and drapery business. In 1787 the Lelant cellars, comprising a newly built quay, wharf and cellars "most advantageously situated for trade, for exports and imports in coals, iron, hemp, timber, tin, copper, and manufactured articles" were to let and the following year John Carne of St.Austell sold his "business in the mercery, drapery and manchester line", a tannery business was to let at Stratton and "the Tontine Assembly and Coffee Rooms" at Truro.

In 1789 a biscuit baking business was sold at Falmouth and mills let at Tresillian "well adapted for carrying on an extensive flour trade" also included a malt-house and bake-house. The same year the "Newkey Cellars" were offered for letting by John Carne and Co., a business "carried on for many years... with great success, the sale of malt, iron, coals, and groceries with a variety of other articles". Two sloops were also for sale. To be let in December was "The House which belong to the New Theatre and Assembly-Rooms in Truro. The taker will have the advantage of furnishing the Assembly with tea and coffee; and if taken by a publican great benefit may be derived from an attendance on the Theatre". In February the following year Mr. Christopher Pennington announced "that in consequence of the decease of his brother, John Pennington, the bellfoundry business will be carried on by him and his son at Stoke Climsland... Orders in the bellfoundry line will be carefully attended to, and punctually executed".

In February 1793 at Par there was to let a "well-accustomed, eligible house and shop, backlets, limekin, coal-house, cellars, deal board yard and a very good walled garden, and every conveniency for carrying on the woollen trade". The deceased Mrs. Emmett and Son had carried on this business "a great number of years... with success, and [it was] now in the possession of Mr. Fox". "Parr is a sea-port where vessels trade from Bristol and London, distant three miles from St.Austell and four from Fowey, and near several prosperous tin works". There was even an incipient tourist trade developing. At Penzance in June 1791 it was reported "Several gentlemen and ladies have lately arrived at Penzance, Marazion, and other places round Mount's Bay; not only for the purpose of sea bathing, but on account of the great salubrity of the air, which has had the most happy effects on persons afflicted by pulmonic disorders".

PUBLIC HOUSES

Evident from the paper and from the many surviving fine inn buildings of this century is the thriving nature of the public house, accomodation, beer and spirit selling businesses in the period. Surveys and meetings were regularly held in public houses and periodically they were advertised for sale and to be let. In September 1781 there was the Ship Inn, Fowey to let, "situated in the market place, together with two very good stables, a barn and garden... Also to be disposed of, all or part of the household furniture, a quantity of spirituous liquors, a quantity of exceeding good hay of last and present year's growth... a very few rich meadows, near to the premises". The following year "that well-accustomed inn called the White Hart [Bodmin]... There are two chaises, eight horses and a great quantity of hay which (with all or any part of the furniture) the taker may have." J.Commins of Penzance appraised "the nobility and gentlemen in general" that he had opened his house, a hotel, inn and coffee-house, "for their reception which is pleasantly situated in the centre of the town, commands an extensive prospect of Mount's Bay, and the country adjacent; the rooms are large and airy, his beds are new, and all other furniture suitable. He has laid in a stock of good wines. Stabling for any number of horses, and a convenient coach house; a post-chaise and able horses with a careful driver. Those who will please favour him with their company may depend on meeting with every civility and attendance to render their accommodation agreeable. He has erected a convenient bathing machine. He desires likewise to acquaint his customers in general, that he still continues his business as a brazier, plumber and tinman as usual. An ordinary every day at one."

In 1783 there was offered for letting the Crown and Sceptre at Lostwithiel "with three stalled stables, a coach house for three carriages and all other necessary conveniences, together with a large garden, orchard and about 33 acres of good meadow ground. Lostwithiel lies in the direct road and about half way from Falmouth to Plymouth and is the nearest turnpike road from Falmouth to London and the said inn is so ancient and well known that particulars are not necessary to recommend it". Samuel Pentecost at the General Wolfe Inn, St.Austell had built an extra apartment and hoped "to merit the favour of the nobility, gentry &c. travelling that way". Thomas Billing Gray of the King's Arms Tavern, Cawsand "(late the sign of the Cawsand Volunteers)" had done the same and hoped for the "favours of the nobility, gentry, travellers and others". Thomas Starmer of the King's Arms, Bodmin had newly taken on that "commodious inn" and James Drew of the White Hart, St.Austell urged support for his successor David Price in 1784. The same year Robert Polsue of Fentonwoon, near Camelford had laid in "a stock of genuine wines and spirituous liquors. Such ladies and gentlemen as shall please honour him with their favours, may depend on being accommodated with good clean beds, and convenient stables, and their favours most gratefully acknowledged... N.B. Fentonwoon is but a short distance from the borough of Camelford, a very agreeable walk; public road leading from the borough to the said inn turns short by the western turnpike-gate, leading to Wadebridge, and about one hundred yards distant from it".

In 1785 a "new-built inn" at Wainhouse Corner was advertised and Samuel Pentecost, junior, of the General Wolfe, St.Austell asked for continued support, he having succeeded his father who had died. William Parks was the new landlord of the Plume of Feathers, Mitchell and the following year Philip Lott had made improvements to his house, the Bedford Inn, Camelford. The Crown and Sceptre, Lostwithiel was to let again in 1786 and Francis Rogers requested support for "that huge, commodious, and old accustomed Inn, called The Ship and Castle, in Penzance, which he has fitted up

Trematon, Castle, Cornwall.

in the genteelest manner, and completely furnished... N.B. An elegant theatre is now erecting in the yard behind the house; and there is a most commodious bathing-house a convenient distance from it".

The King's Head Inn in Redruth was for sale in January 1787 and in the summer following the death of her husband Mary Prockter of the White Hart Inn, Launceston requested the support of her customers in the future - "she intends continuing the business as usual". In 1788 T.Williams of the Royal Standard Hotel, Falmouth said he was about to "discontinue the innkeeping business... [he] takes this opportunity to thank his numerous friends for their past favours, and to hope a continuance of them whilst he remains in the business". In 1789 Samuel Branton had taken on the King's Arms, Redruth and the landlord of the Crimmel Passage Inn had "lately altered and much improved his house, also new furnished the lodging rooms in a very handsome manner... The house pleasantly situated near Mount Edgcumbe. the passage boats are good and safe, and manned with careful and sober men. N.B. Over Crimmel Passage is the shortest way to Falmouth and the Land's End, through Liskeard, Lostwithiel, St.Austle and Truro." The King's Arms, Wadebridge was to let for six years or more. The house had a brewhouse and four stables and all stock was to be disposed of including "all brewing utensils". In September there died suddenly Mr. Harbin of the Greyhound Inn, Liskeard - "his character was generally esteemed, and his conduct and behaviour irreproachable". In October "that well accutomed inn, situate at Camborne, known by the sign of the King's Head" was offered for letting.

In 1790 the notice about the Crimmel Passage Inn was repeated with the starred addition "A new bathing machine, and a good beach, at all times of tide". The London Inn, Redruth was to be let for a term of years to be agreed on and the remainder of the lease of 99 years on "two young good lives" of the Ship Inn, Mevagissey was offered for sale - the "inn is large, commodious, and well-accustomed; conveniently situated in the Market-place; and has been the principal inn in Mevagissey for fifty years past". Thomas Hugoe had opened the new-built house, the Prince George Inn, at Camborne and welcomed customers. It had "a Chaise, with able horses and careful drivers". Robert Pape was giving up the White Hart Inn, Bodmin on account of his wife's ill health. He offered it for letting. "It consists of every accomodation necesarry for carrying on an extensive business; has good stabling behind, and has the constant run of the Falmouth coach, which passes through Bodmin three times a wek". William Roberts of the Crown Inn, Lostwithiel thanked customers for their support, "which in a house newly opened by him has far exceeded his expectations". It was then to be let. New tenants at the Queen's Head Inn on the West Bridge, Truro (Richard Perry) and the Crown Inn, Lostwithiel (Francis Leavers) welcomed support in 1792.

SHIPPING

The pubs in the small Cornish ports derived benefit from the traffic by sea and no doubt some of the liquor they sold was illegally obtained. While trade by land was clearly growing with the establishment of turnpike roads and the use of packhorses, waggons etc. much was still sea-borne. Notices of ships for sale, often illustrated with nice little sketches of boats were a regular feature of the Sherborne Mercury. Most were small vessels but occasionally there were bigger ones, often prizes from the wars waged during the period against France and others. "For sale by the candle" at the George Inn, Padstow on 27th January 1782 was the Mary "about 250 tons, lately arrived from Jamaica, a prime sailor, square stern. French built and well found having had a considerable repair before her last trip. Well adapted for any service where a ship of her size is required".

The brig, the Cornish Oak, burthen 140 tons was offered for sale in February 1783 at the Red Lion, Truro - "now lying at the Newham Quay. Built about 12 months ago by John Bone of Padstow, on account of her easy draught of water, swift sailing, and excellent order and condition, one of the most desirable vessels of her burthen of any in England." On 10th March the same year at the King's Arms tavern on the Strand, Falmouth "the new French built ship Le Keizer, taken on her passage from L'Orient and Brest to the Isle of France by his Majesty's frigate, La Prudente... A prime sailer, square stern, figure head, burthen 325 tons, carpenter's measurement. Was built at Havre de Grace, sheathed on the stocks and launched in October 1781. She is a strong built ship; her timber, beams, knees &c. are of large scantling, composed of the best materials, and well put together; in short, she is a handsome, well-built, and complete merchant ship, fit for the West Indies, Mediterranean, or any other trade where burthen and dispatch are required". Ten Dutch ships were taken by the Dolphin and Grace private ships of war of Penzance in 1780 and 1781 and four years later accounts regarding their disposal were still being sorted out. In 1787 a Danish brigantine was sold at Penzance, in 1789 a French brig of 160 tons on the Isles of Scilly, in 1790 a Danish brig at Falmouth.

There was to be sold at Falmouth in December 1784 "the good brig Vulture; burthen about 180 tons; plantation built; two years and a half old; with two decks, one of which was laid in the port of Falmouth last summer; well found in stores of all kinds; fit for any trade where despatch is required, and may be sent to sea at a very small expence; now lying at Falmouth, and there to be delivered". A vessel probably to be used as a privateer was advertised in 1785 at Falmouth, "a lugger, about 59 feet keel, and 20 feet beam; pierced for 16 guns; strong built, and a remarkable fast sailing vessel. She has 14 double fortified six-pounders, with carriages &c. which may be had with or without the vessel".

Two years later a boat builder at Little Falmouth advertised "a new vessel, ready for launching; burthen in tones, 170; supposed to carry from 220 to 230 tons. She has a carved head, quarter-pieces, and tarssail. She is not mailed but is well calculated for a ship, loow(?) or brig; and has been four years in building". There were boat builders in other ports. In 1790 John Roberts of Helford offered for sale "the good sloop Diligence; burthen per register 60, will carry 100 tons; a remarkable fast sailer; was built by the owner for his own use in the port of Gweek, and exceeding good workmanship put in her." The same year Joseph Hooper, shipbuilder, had for sale a "very fine new sloop, now lying on the stocks at Torpoint, of the burthen of 50 tons or thereabouts". A clinchwork built vessel was for sale by Thomas Shepheard, builder, at Mevagissey in February 1793, "now on the stocks; 51 feet long by the keel; 19 feet beam; about 87 tons measurement; a strong well built vessel; and calculated in every respect for fast sailing; will be ready to launch in or about three weeks, sooner if required". A new cutter was for sale at Boyers Cellars the same month, burthen about 45 tons. Further particulars from Peter Smith, shipwright. In September 1792 a new sloop, "burthen 40 tons, strongly built, will last well, and fit for any employ" was offered by John Wilcock, shipwright, of Fowey and in the summer of 1793 a "very fine, strong, clench work vessel, which will be ready to launch in a few days... about 150 tons; is calculated either for a cutter or lugger; by appearances will sail remarkably fast, and will make a compleat cruizer; pierced for 20 guns. Apply to Ninian Douglas, Fowey."

In 1788 were sold two vessels that had formerly been in service with the Customs, the Hawke, lying at Little Falmouth, 65' 3" long, 21 feet 2" broad, 9 feet deep in the hold, and the Squirrel at Looe, "near seven years old; a square sterned vessel; clinch work (built by Mr. Parkin, of Cawsand). Her length from the fore-part of the main stern to the after-part of the stern port aloft, 68 feet 2 inches; her breath 20 feet 1 inch; depth in the hold, 9 feet 6 inches; and in 110 tons, carpenter's measurement; an exceeding fast sailer, and may be easily converted into a cutter or a brig, and fit for an employ where dispatch is required". Also for sale from time to time a variety of barges, cutters, some "well calculated for the Guernsey trade", luggers, sloops, brigantines, yachts, barks.

SHIPWRECKS

The hazardous nature of shipping is brought out by the references to periodic shipwrecks. The goods salvaged provide evidence of what ships were trading in at the time. In January 1782 there was a sale of 44 barrels of good Irish Beef, at the house of Robert Blundstone, innkeeper, Truro, part of the cargo saved from the St.John Baptist sloop lately stranded in Porth Island bay, Cubert. "The night of 5th February [1782] we had [at Falmouth] a most violent gale of wind from the east which forced three packet boats and some other vessels on shore and did considerable damage to the shipping in the harbour." It was in this gale that Indiamen were dismasted near the Scillies. In April 1784 six tons of gallipoli oil was sold from the Floreat Commercium, from Gallipoli to Amsterdam, stranded in Mount's Bay in November. On the 20th March 1786 there was "discovered lying on Cudgewy Rocks, on the east point of Porthpean... the Prussian ship

De Benconkorb, of 500 tons... with mast, baulk, staves &c. from Stettin to Bordeaux". Fortunately through the efforts of local men she was "got off and warped into this pier" (Mevagissey). She was repaired there and managed to renew her voyage in late July. In December 1787 "the stern, quarter-deck, bowspirits and part of the boom of a large sloop were found at this place [Mevagissey]. On examining, found the name on the stern to be the Two Brothers, of Weymouth. It is supposed she must have foundered at sea, the wind blowing a heavy gale at east". At Falmouth the same gale caused the Greyhound packet boat to part from one of her cables and a brig from her anchors, damaging another vessel, laden and about to set sail for Marseilles. The Princess Mary, from London to Jamaica, put into Falmouth having lost her foremast and the Eagle revenue cutter was driven on shore in Mounts Bay, the crew being saved but the vessel lost. In March 1788 masts, yards, shrouds, cables and anchors, other cordage and furniture of the Duke of Cornwall, lately wrecked on Scilly, were sold at Penzance.

On 27th November 1789 Nicholas Bennett, sadler, and Peter Dowe, seaman, set out from St.Ives in an open lugsail boat for St.Agnes but were never heard of again. "The last time the boat was seen was about four o'clock in the afternoon, near the rocks called the Stones, off St.Ives Bay, beating to windward". The Thynne packet boat, Captain Wolf, arrived at Falmouth on 22nd November 1790 "with mails, from New York and Halifax. Mr. Joseph Brailey, the master, and six other persons, were unfortunately washed over-board and drowned on the 5th instant". On the 3rd February 1791 a vessel was driven on shore and wrecked at St. Minver. "A great number of people immediately proceeded to the spot, where they found a fine new copper-bottomed schooner of about 80 tons, named the Friendship of London, under a high cliff, supposed to be driven on shore some time in the preceeding night, without a living soul on board; two men only were found drowned in the hold. It cannot be conjectured what is become of the rest of the crew, as the boat hath not been seen or heard of". In February 1792 "the Carolina... from London for Cork and the West Indies, with Government stores, was driven on shore at Coverack... and entirely lost. The captain, crew and some passengers were saved, but three men belong to Coverack, who went to the assistance of the persons on board the Carolina, were drowned."

Tin continued to be sent by sea to London and in 1785 the owners and masters of five tin ships, the Polly, the Furly, the Spackman, the Prince of Wales and the Duke of Cornwall, gave notice that they would not be responsible for any goods destroyed by fire, stolen or damaged on their ships unless the same happened to be the fault of their masters or crew. Links with Bristol are indicated by the sale of the good sloop Sisters in August 1793, "has been for some time past employed in a constant trade from Bristol to Falmouth, in which trade the purchaser may have an opportunity of still keeping her". References were regularly made to other ships being suitable for the coasting trade, trade to Guernsey, to the Mediterranean, Newfoundland etc.

The start of the passenger traffic to America is suggested by the advert of the American Ship, Birmingham, about 300 tons burthen, for Baltimore in April 1793, "now lying at Falmouth, is ready to receive goods and passengers on moderate terms, and will sail in about eight days. Said ship has good accomodation for passengers."

SMUGGLING

The 1780s appear to have been a highpoint of smuggling in Cornwall. An ancestor of mine, Jacob Whetter, was arrested for receiving smuggled kegs of spirits at Benhurden, Gorran. The revenue men arrived at the farm in the early morning and found his horses sweating. Alerted by their arrival he poured the kegs of spirits into the pig salt but his ruse was detected and he served six months in goal at Bodmin. The type of goods being smuggled is indicated by the regular sales of "Customed goods", often in large quantities, brandy, geneva, red port wine, sherry wine at St.Ives in June 1783. Added to this rum in August. In February 1787 as well as spirits and wine, "fine black tea" was offered for sale. Falmouth was another port where regular sales were held. In December 1791 for instance as well as alcohol tea, coffee, currants, cotton, silks, salt and satin were to be sold.

Men were often charged at the assizes with offences connected with smuggling. In August 1787 William Daw was said to have assaulted and obstructed Christopher Childs, officer of excise, in the execution of his duty and was ordered to remain in confinement. In August 1791 William Moyle was convicted for killing a mare the property of Daniel Bartlett. Moyle was "a smuggler, Daniel Bartlett... an excise officer; and it appeared that the prisoner had committed this offence out of revenge to the officer, who had little before seized some smuggled goods belonging to the prisoner." In August 1792 "Thomas Woolcock was found guilty of having assaulted Richard Corfield, an excise officer, in the execution of his office."

There was a case in August 1789 "the decision of which must materially affect the smuggling business... The plaintiffs, some of whom live in Cornwall and others in Guernsey, ship at Guernsey to the order and risk of the defendants, residents in Cornwall, several large quantities of spirituous liquors and teas; the liquors are shipped in half anchors and 'flings', clearly, as the learned Judge observed, for the greater ease of smuggling them." The judge found that the venders "being subjects of his Majesty, and in sound policy ought not to be permitted to support contracts which in their effects are so injurious to the revenue of this country. The plaintiff's counsel desired a special case for the opinion of the court of King's Bench, which was granted".

Ships were regularly advertised for sale as good for the "Guernsey trade". The work of the customs boats, the Hawke and Squirrel, was referred to before their sale in 1788. The Hawke brought into Falmouth in February 1786 a large cutter, the Two Brothers. She "had on board when she was seized, 500 ankers of brandy and gin, 75 boxes of tea, about 20 tons of tea, some nankeens, cards, &c. &c. Her cargo is estimated at £8000 value". In November 1787 the Squirrel was in Cawsand bay one night when it was boarded by a large smuggling cutter, believed to be the Experiment of

Guernsey, mounting 14 guns, with a crew of 40 men. The customs officers were taken on board the cutter and confined in the cabin. Her cargo were transferred to boats of the place and landed and later the customs men were released. In February the following year the commissioners of his Majesty's Customs offered £50 reward for information that would lead to the conviction of the offenders.

In December 1787 some people carrying a large quantity of wool from Tregony to Looe were stopped by Mr. Hill, riding officer at Polmear who found that the packs of wool were not marked as they should be. The wool was taken to the customs house at Fowey and the matter considered by the commissioners of the Customs. In February 1788 a large quantity of brandy and geneva was seized at Falmouth together with a boat marked "John Vigurse Gerran" by officers at the port. Afterwards the boat was rescued by person or persons unknown. The commissioners offered a reward of £20 for information that would lead to the conviction of the offenders. A similar thing happened the following month. On the evening of 19th March 1788 "some person or persons unknown feloniously stole from the Custom House Key of this port, a small open boat, which had on the preceding day been seized, and deposited at the said key". £10 was offered for information. In June 1789 Lieut. Gabriel Bray of the revenue schooner, the Hind, based at Fowey, whose field of operations extended from Portland to St.Ives Bay advertised for information "of goods about to be illegally landed, or where sunk ready for landing". He promised to conceal the identity of people giving such information who would receive "one third share of the seizure money, besides a present over and above out of his own pocket... should any person residing near there, who cannot write, wish to give him regular informations, Lieutenant Bray can shew such person a method of correspondence with him just as clear and intelligible as writing, if the person will only wait on Lieutenant Bray, at his house in Fowey, for a few minutes".

In late August 1791 the customs house boat on Scilly was rowed late at night close to a smuggling vessel, laden with contraband goods in Old Grimsby Harbour, near Tresco. The crew of the smuggling vessel fired repeatedly into the customs house boat so that two revenue men were killed, John Oliver and William Millet, and another, John Jane, seriously wounded. The inquest arrived at the verdict of wilful murder. "The smuggling vessel got off. The excise officers were well respected and have left large families". The vessel was later identified as the Friendship of Penzance, belonging to James Dunkin, and commanded by George Branwell. The commissioners offered a reward of £500 for the arrest of Dunkin who fired a gun and pardons to men who assisted this and gave information about others involved in the shooting, the successful identification being rewarded with a further £200.

Writing from Plymouth on 23rd May 1792 - "Arrived his Majesty's ship Andromeda, Capt. Salisbury, from a cruize off the Dodman; she captured a small pleasure yacht called the Nymph, belonging to Guernsey, laden with 60 ankers of spirits, and brought her into this port". In May 1793 a small revenue cutter saw a vessel between Land's End and Scilly during the day, "at such a distance, however, as to preclude any chance of coming up with her before night". The commander "declined to give chase, but supposing her to be an English smuggler, and that she might probably be met with in the night under the land, discharging her cargo, the cutter bore away upon that speculation luckily, and before the morning was close alongside before the enemy were aware of her approach". Capt. John shifted four guns to the side next to the boat and hailed her. Finding she was French "in a peremptory tone threatened to sink her in an instant, unless she immediately struck, which she accordingly did, apprehending that her force was greatly inferior to the cutter". It turned out that the vessel was a French privateer "well equipped with small arms, and well qualified for the business, although she had been out 18 days and taken nothing".

INLAND TRANSPORT

While much of Cornwall's trade went by sea, inland transport was developing, aided in this period by the establishment of turnpike roads. Regular advertisements appeared for the letting of the various turnpikes, Helston, Penryn and Redruth, Launceston, Saltash, St.Austell to Lostwithiel, Liskeard, Bodmin, Tregony, Callington and others. Some turnpike houses survive beside Cornish roads, small buildings abutting roads here and there; many have been removed. Placenames record some, notably St.Blazey Gate on the St.Austell to Lostwithiel road. Undoubtedly their construction gave a boost to horse and carriage traffic and to inns and hotels in their vicinity.

Regular carriage services came to be established. In 1783 a new service was announced - "a new and elegant Diligence between Exeter and Falmouth, through Oakhampton, Launceston, Bodmin and Truro, sets out from the London Inn, Exeter, every Monday, Wednesday and Friday, and from the King's Arms, Falmouth; will continue to run alternately every other day from each of the above inns, and carry passengers at £1.11s.6d... These Diligences stop the night at the White Hart, Bodmin, going down, and at the White Hart, Launceston, coming up, and arrive at Falmouth and Exeter, early in the forenoon." At Exeter they met similar Diligences to London, Bath, Bristol, Southampton and Oxford. By 1787 mail coaches with a guard provided by the government were running between Exeter every morning at 3 a.m. and the King's Arms Hotel, Falmouth every morning at 8 a.m. They stopped at "Mr. Cartwright's, the White Hart, Oakhampton; Mrs. Prockter's, the White Hart, Launceston; Mr. Pape's, the White Hart, Bodmin and at Mr. Rivera's the King's Head, Truro". In September that year another "entire new and elegant Diligence, well guarded, will set out from Thompson's Hotel, Exeter at 3 a.m. and continue to run every Monday, Wednesday and Friday to Falmouth in 16 hours, and from Williams's Hotel, Falmouth every Tuesday and Saturday at the same hour and return to Exeter in the same time... Will change horses at the following regular stages, where chaises and able horses may be had at the shortest notice, viz. Fountain, Oakhampton; White Horse, Lifton; King's Arms, Launceston; London Inn, Five-Lanes; King's Arms, Bodmin; Red Lion, Truro." There was clearly some rivalry between the various services. Carriages also left Thompson's hotel every

St Germains Priory, Cornwall. Pl. 1

day for Salisbury, Gosport, London, Bath, Bristol, Oxford, Plymouth, Dock i.e. the future Devonport and Barnstaple.

In November 1790 an alternate day service was in operation from Blundstone's new hotel, Falmouth to the London Inn, Exeter, setting off in the morning at 6 a.m. The advert headed "Falmouth and Exeter Coach" probably related to the same service in being in 1783. The hire of smaller carriages was regulated at a meeting at the King's Head, Truro on 28th April 1791 - "At a meeting held this day, by public advertisement, we the undermentioned innkeepers came to the following resolution: That in compliance with the witnesses of the public at large, we have agreed to charge, as usual, One shilling per mile for chaise and pair of horses. We return our sincere thanks for past favours, and hope by utmost attention to please to ensure a continuance. Robert Blunstone, Falmouth. Ann Rivers, Truro. Francis Symons, Indian Queens. Robert Pape, Bodmin. Mary Prockter, Launceston".

The use of wagons and carts on the roads was carefully controlled. In October 1790 there was an announcement in the Sherborne Mercury, headed "A Caution to Drivers of Waggons, Carts, &c." "Whereas I John Cocker, of the parish of St.Nyott, have been convicted of not having had any person either on foot or on horseback to guide a waggon which I was driving on the King's highway, on Friday the 1st day of this month. I do hereby thank the lenity of the Magistrate before whom I was convicted, for having remitted so much of the penalty as the law admits, to which I was liable for the said offence, on condition of my making this public acknowledgement. The Mark of John Cocker. Boconnoc Parsonage, October 9, 1790." Having horses for hire was also subject to conditions. In January 1788 John Hancock was convicted of having let horses to hire, without issuing a post-horse ticket, according to the directions of the Act of the 25th George III called the Post Horse Act. The penalty was £10 but the informer on Mr. Hancock requested the mayor mitigate the penalty to £5, he giving up his reward for the same. Mr. Hancock made his submission in the paper and promised "to act more conscientiously in future; I have thought it proper, by this public advertisement, to acknowledge the lenity that has been shown me, and hope that this will be a means of deterring other innkeepers from such practices in future." In a N.B. item "Mr. James Hodge, the farmer of the post-horse duties of district No. 15, the said prosecutor for the above offence, was induced to request the said mitigation, merely because his farm had not commenced, but immediately declared his fixed resolution in future, was to press for the levying of the full penalty."

BRIDGES AND PAVEMENTS

Attention was being paid to other aspects of the transport infrastructure. In July 1793 tenders were invited for the rebuilding of Tideford bridge. Plans could be inspected at the Rev. Penwarne's, St.Germans and the Bridge-Warden, J.Symons, was to consider the tenders at a meeting at the King's Arms in the village on 19th August.

The work was to be completed by the following October. A new ferry carrying foot passengers, carriages, horses and cattle between Plymouth Dock and Torpoint started on Monday 4th July 1791 - "proper and convenient boats, manned by able and careful seamen, will be constantly ready to accommodate all travellers desirous of passing to and from the adjacent parts of the counties of Devon and Cornwall. It is perhaps unnecessary to add that this passage opens a shorter and much easier communication between Plymouth-Dock and the western part of Cornwall than any now in use; and the proprietors are determined that no attention or expence shall be waiting to render the attendance punctual, and the accommodation complete."

In towns the needs of pedestrians was catered for. At Truro in September 1790 "all persons who are desirous to contract for laying the pitched pavement of the streets of the said borough are requested to send sealed tenders for the same to Mr. William Jenney, attorney at law, within the said borough, before ten o'clock, on Tuesday the 28th instant". Damage was inflicted on some structures by vandalism. In July 1793 - "Whereas some evil disposed person, or persons, has of late wantonly and repeatedly broke down and much damaged the parapet walls of Grampound bridge, this is therefore to give notice, that any person giving information to Samuel Hext, clerk of the roads for the county of Cornwall, or to John Truscott, surveyor of bridges for the western division of the said county, so as the offender, or offenders may be convicted thereof, shall immediately upon such conviction, received a reward of five guineas."

NEW HOUSES

Descriptions of houses for sale give some idea of how richer members of society lived. On 27th August 1783 there was held at Mr. Blight's inn, Truro a sale of "all that handsome modern built dwelling house situate in the Cross, Truro wherein Thomas Heyes esq., deceased, lately lived, now in the possession of Leigh Dickinson esq., whose term therein expires the 29th September 1784, consisting of two parlours, a drawing room and breakfast room, with a proportionable number of bed-chambers, an excellent kitchen, servants hall, and scullery all within the principal building. The other offices, such as brew-house, wash-house, laundry, cellars &c. are detached from the house; and behind the whole is a spacious walled garden, extending to the river." The possession of nice views was clearly a good selling point. To be sold or rented in 1784 was a "new-built house, just about the turnpike-gate at Saltash, with four rooms on a floor, and two light closets on the upper floors; a cellar, wash-house, and a large garden behind the house, and a small field in front of it. It commands a delightful view of the ships in the Hamoaze, Mount Edgcumbe, the Dock-yard, and town of Dock, from the front of the house; and from the bow windows behind it, a most extensive view of the rivers and country to the northward of it".

Also at Truro in 1788 was to be let "a commodious dwelling-house, situated at Truro Vean, by the parish of St.Clements, within a quarter of a mile of the borough of

Truro, fit for the immediate reception of a gentleman's family; consisting of two parlours, kitchen, pantry, dairy, cellar, wash kitchen, stable, other outhouses, and a large courtlage, four lodging rooms, and a closet on the first floor, and two garrets, with a garden in front." With some properties in the old boroughs went voting rights. At Saltash in 1789 was to be sold "all that dwelling house and garden, together with a stable thereto adjoining, situate in Fore Street... and all that adjoining dwelling house and garden, with the Malthouse thereto belonging, now in the possession of Mr. Worth... The above premises are two burgages; each of which, according to the right of voting lately contended for, will qualify a purchaser to vote in the choice of representatives in parliament of the said borough".

At Marazion "a large and elegant stone-built Mansion-house... (lately occupied by J.M.Chadwicke, Esq. deceased, and now by the Right Honourable the Earl of Donegal)" was to be let for term of years in 1790. "The house is in perfectly good repair, and consists of a dining room 22 feet 9 by 17 feet 2 inches; two parlours; a drawing-room, elegantly finished, 21 feet 8 by 17 feet 8 inches; eight bed-chambers, with dressing rooms; together with a large kitchen, servants hall, pantry, dairy, wine and beer cellars, &c. &c. on the ground floor. Adjoining are offices, coach-house, good stables, with yards, &c. and a dog-kennel; and behind and in front of the house are neat shrubberies. A large walled garden well stocked with fruit trees, and having a compleat hot-house together with a large kitchen garden, belong to the premises. In every respect the house and premises are admirably adapted to the convenient and elegant situation of a genteel family".

In 1792 was to be let "all that excellent modern-built commodious dwelling-house, called Penmount House, situate in the parish of St. Clements, within two miles of the town of Truro... with attached and detached offices, gardens, and plantations, together with 214 acres of meadow, pasture, and arable land. The house is situated on an easy eminence, commanding extensive and beautiful prospects of the sea and the adjacent rich country, and contains two complete suites of apartments of the ground and first story, with suitable servants' chamber, hall, vestibule, principal and back stair-cases, a spacious kitchen, with useful connected offices, servants' hall, and cellarage."

SERVANTS

It can be seen that for their households to function a large number of servants and other employees were required. Adverts for servants frequently appeared in the columns of the Sherborne Mercury - in 1781 Edward Giddy of Truro, "wanted in a gentleman's family near Truro, a footman and a lady's maid who can dress hair and also a good cook maid." The following year Stephen Ustick of Falmouth, mercer, wrote that "good wages [would be] given to a steady, sober, servant man, who can wait at table and take care of a horse." Mr. Michell in Helston in 1783 required "A middle-aged woman cook, who is capable of acting as housekeeper in a gentleman's family who reside in the country. Likewise a footman who perfectly understands his business... None need apply but those who can produce unexceptionable characters from their last places." The same year "a servant who has been used to taking care of horses and drives a postchaise" was wanted at Nance, near Redruth and in 1785 the Rev. Robert Walker of St. Winnow required "a servant to take care of horses, and to work in a garden." A little later - "Wanted for a gentleman in Cornwall, a good groom, who also understands somewhat of hunting and to take care of a few harriers, and to wait at table occasionally. N.B. None need apply but those who can have an undeniable good character from his last place. Enquire of the printers of this paper, or of Mr. Norway, at Lostwithiel." In 1791 a woman servant was required at Tregony for a "country clergyman's family, which consists of five gentlefolks, and four servants; she must understand cookery well, and superintend the other three servants. A good character will be expected."

Compared with the sophisticated accommodation that the upper strata occupied lesser folk were no doubt more interested in the kind of property leased for 99 years on three lives at Paul in 1787 - "17 dwelling houses, 15 closes of very rich pasture land, and several tofts, and small garden plots, all situate in the near the towns of Paul and Mousehole". But of these there was little more description.

WORKHOUSES

The poor, people with disabilities and the aged may have been forced to live in the workhouses and poorhouses that were then established. There has already been noticed the advertisement in 1781 for a master of the Bodmin workhouse, "a middle aged man who is acquainted with the business of a rug-maker, or any other branch of the woollen manufactory and can be well recommended. A good salary can be given". Applicants were to apply to the overseers of the town by letter or in person. In 1786 the overseers in the parish of Falmouth complained that it had "suffered considerably by paupers having been removed to that parish who appear to belong to the town of Falmouth". They entreated J.P.s in their examination of paupers "carefully to distinguish... which they belong to; the same being separate and distinct places of settlement". The following year the town of Falmouth was looking for a governor of their poorhouse - "Wanted, to take the charge and government of the poor in the poor-house... a steady, sober, and industrious, middle-aged man, who is married, and a person skilled in the twine-spinning or woollen manufactory, as it is intended the paupers shall all be employed in one of the aforesaid branches. Such a person, willing to undertake the above charges, and producing a good character from the principal inhabitants where he resides, will meet with encouragement by applying to the churchwardens and overseers of the poor of the town... either personally or by letter". The churchwardens and overseers of the poor of the parish of Kenwyn advertised in 1791 that they had in the poorhouse four children, "from 10 to 15 years of age, which they will bind out as apprentices with suitable premiums, to any persons of good character who carry on trades, whereby the said apprentices may be enabled to get their living".

RUNAWAYS

The apprenticing of young paupers to employers did not always work out satisfactorily and a regular crop of runaways was noted in the columns of the paper, many specifically described as "parish apprentices" - Peter Prout, who left his master, Joseph Cardew of Liskeard in early 1784. Aged about 19 years; had on when he went away a brown coat, nankeen waistcoat and breeches; he was about five feet seven inches high; had an impediment in his speech, was knee-capped, and a little hard of hearing. Thomas Grylls, of Landulph, who left James Rowter the same year, about twenty years of age, five feet six inches high, dark complexion, and a "down look"; wore away a double-breasted blue broad-cloth coat, red waistcoat, and blue breeches. "If he will immediately return to his master he will be kindly received and all past offences forgiven". Nicholas Harvey, who left Edward Hugoe in 1785; he was about 20 years of age, about five feet nine inches high, of a fair complexion and wore his own light hair; he carried off with him two coats, one of a dark brown colour, the other of a light coloured beaver. Joseph Sambells, left Alexander Moon, of Trematon, in St. Stephens next Saltash on Monday 4th April 1785. He was about 17 years of age, four feet six inches high, "set made", dark complexion, and curled hair; wore away a brown coat, blue plush breeches and black stockings. In July the same year William Martin, went from John Caddy, yeoman, of the parish of St.Martin in Meneage. He was about eleven years of age, about four feet high, of a fair complexion, and flaxen coloured curled hair. James Stephens left his master James Hill, stay-maker, of Helston on Thursday 27th October 1785. He was 19 years of age, about 5 feet and 3 inches high, of a dark complexion, dark-brown eyes, and wore his own (dark) hair, in loose curls; was rather a stout make, and very broad over the shoulders. Wore away a blue cloth coat, with plain yellow metal buttons, and waistcoat, with chintz trimming, and nankeen breeches. In the spring of 1786 Charles Borlase ran away from his master, John Williams of St. Austell. He was 19 years of age, about five feet four inches high, brown complexion, dark hair, and lame on his left leg; wore away a lead colour coat, white waistcoat and black breeches. Thomas Marrish ran away, the 26th of June 1787, from his master, William Ivey, of St.Merryn, aged 18 years, healthy complexion, black short hair; wore away a black cloth waistcoat and drab cloth breeches, and carried off a mixed great coat belonging to his master.

Mary Ann Hoskin ran away from her master, George Bennats of Gulval on 21st June 1789. She was about 14 years of age, with brown coloured hair, fair face; wore off a striped dowlas bed-gown, a brown cloth coat, black hat and no cap. John Rose and Sarah Popplestone ran away from William Goad, farmer, of St.Stephens in early 1792. The boy was aged about 18, "with light hair, five feet four inches high, pock-marked, and round favoured." The girl, 19, "dark complexion, blackish hair, pretty stout and thick made". Later in the year, Matthew Johns, a labourer, ran away from his parish of St.Just in Roseland. He was about "21 years of age, pretty stout, about five feet ten, of a brown complexion, and wears his own brown hair". Whoever apprehended him and conveyed him back to the overseers of the poor of the parish would receive five guineas reward.

It will be seen that the "runaway" evidence provides a unique look at a cross-section of the young people at the time, at least spirited ones among the lower classes, their physical appearance - perhaps useful for medical-genetic researchers, also for those interested in the clothes fashion of the time. Other runaways I noted at this time were in 1782 Robert Hambly who left a carpenter in Luxulyan "about 18, dark complexion, 5'6", strait dark brown hair"; Thomas Evan, originally belonging to the Carmarthenshire militia and from Carmarthen, who left a Lostwithiel carpenter "21, 5'8", a well-looking young man, with strait black hair, had on a blue jacket and hog-skin breeches"; in 1783 Richard Rodda, who left a shoemaker of St.Columb Major "5'6", wore away a brown coat, has black hair tied, of a thin make"; Ann Stephens, who left a yeoman from Manaccan "14, of short stature and much marked with the small pox"; Thomas Tallick, who left his master at Polkerris "about 18, brown complexion, straight hair, 5'7", wore away a blue coat, flowered linen waistcoat and corduroy breeches"; in 1784 John Bosavern left a house-carpenter, at Talland "about five feet eight inches high, round favoured, pale complexion, brown curled hair, black eyebrows, a large foot, and one large ankle. Had on when he went off a new dark plain cloth coat, yellow dimity waistcoat, and light corded breeches"; Richard Henwood left a blacksmith at St.Neot, "about 19 years of age, five feet four or five inches high, strong made, of a fair complexion, goes a little bow-legged, and wears his hair curled"; in 1785 Thomas Mitchell left his master at Lanivet "aged 19 years, of a pale complexion, and brown hair; wore away a brown coat and waistcoat, and striped breeches, with a few fore-part. He is about 5'7" high"; George Hill left his mistress in St.Kew, "about 17 years of age, thick made, about five feet 3 inches high, straight light hair, of a red complexion; wore away a light blue coat, red waistcoat, striped with white and buff breeches; also carried away with him a dark cloth coat, three waistcoats, two red and one everlasting, and pair of Holland-duck breeches, and other clothes of different sorts"; Hill ran away again in 1787, his description then slightly different "in the 20th year of his age, thick made, about five feet and half high, straight light hair, and of a red complexion. He carried away three coats, one deep blue, one light blue, and one of a dark colour; waistcoats of different sorts, and dark fustian breeches; also three shirts, one holland, and two canvas"; Burgess Welman left his clothier master at Fowey, "about 20 years of age, five feet high, strait brown hair, looks red in the face, and pock-marked. He wore away a deep blue coat, black waistcoat, and yellow cloth breeches"; Nicholas Rowe left his master, a mason, of Lanivet "about 23 years of age, 5 feet 5 inches high, of a fair complexion, and black curled hair; wore away a snuff coloured cloth coat, corduroy breeches and a figured velveret waistcoat".

27

In 1790 Joseph Wheeler left his master in St.Blazey, "aged nineteen years, dark brown hair; he is slight and tall, and his right knee much crooked; had on when he went off two blanketing waistcoats, and tinner's boots"; Thomas Congdon left his master in St.Neot, "aged about 13 years, about four feet six inches high, dark complexion, set made, light hair untied; had on went he went off, a striped serge waistcoat, and short canvas trowsers, with other apparel"; Benjamin Hancock left his master, a shipwright at East Looe, wearing "a blue jacket, and black breeches; he is about 18 years of age, and about five feet seven inches high, light brown hair tied behind, and has a dimple in one of his cheeks"; John Pike from his master, a cordwainer at Falmouth, "a short lad, about sixteen years of age, much pock-marked, and has black hair". In 1792 John Hawken left his master, a yeoman at Luxulyan, "aged 19 years and 9 months, about five feet six inches high, of a fair complexion, light hair and yellow at the tip, his right lag is larger than the other. He wore away a blue beaver coat with white metal buttons, and a mixed green coat, with yellow buttons, two waistcoats, one of speckled jean, and the other white cloth, two pair of breeches, one corderoy, and the other plush, with two shirts"; Richard Oates from a peruke maker at Penzance, "about five feet [?] inches high, stout made, pale complexion, dark hair tied, and about 17 years of age"; Edward Roberts from his master at Trerice, Newlyn, "about four feet high, has brown hair, and about twelve years of age"; Jonathan Mark from his master at Luxulyan, "aged 19, about 5 feet 8 or 9 inches high, pale complexion, straight brown hair, slight make, a little round shouldered". In 1793 James Searle left his master in Quethiock, "about 5 feet 8 inches high, of a brown complexion, with long dark hair; wore away a brown coat, a velveret waistcoat, and corduroy breeches"; Thomas Francis, his master, a cordwainer at Mitchell, "about five feet six inches high, dark brown hair, a round and red complexion" and John King, his, at Calengia in St.Hillary, "between 16 and 17 years of age, five feet high, flaxen-hair, and of a very dark complexion. He wore off a blue coat and waistcoat, black breeches, and black stockings."

The evidence is interesting for the light it sheds on disabilities, smallpox marks being common, injured legs etc. People in different parts of Cornwall often seem to have distinctive physical traits, some of which are still observable and these are probably reflected in these descriptions. It was interesting that Richard Rodda who left his master in 1783 was of a "thin make". My great-grandmother was a Rodda and she too was on the thin side, a characteristic which I seem to have inherited. People's hair styles are of interest, some tied back in the 1990s fashion. In one case it was noted that a man wore his own hair, showing that wigs were still common at this period. Clothes were sometimes bright and colourful, this in contrast to the more sombre dress worn by males in the Victorian and later period.

Reftormel Caftle Cornwal.

SCHOOLS

The children of the better off are generally not so well described as the "runaways". They may have attended the numerous local schools in existence by this time. Following the death of the master a replacement was required in October 1789 for the school at Launceston, one "who understands English grammatically, writing, and arithmetick. The late master, who died a few days since, had upwards of sixty scholars at the time of his decease". It seems to have been a boom time for women's education and Elizabeth Stokes opened a school on Ladyday 1790, at Molinnick, near St.Germans.

At Saltash Mrs. Northcote, a widow of a navy surgeon, started a boarding school for young ladies in August 1783. Parents and guardians were assured that for children put under her care "every attention will be paid to their conduct and morals, assisted by a teacher from one of the first schools in London". The school premises were "a commodious, large, airy and well-adapted house for that purpose at the head of Saltash". Among subjects taught were "English grammatically, embroidery, tambour and every other kind of needlework, dancing, drawing, writing and arithmetic, French." Fees were £15 a term which included "washing, tea and sugar" and there were one or two extras. Day scholars were also taken. It appears Mrs. Northcote subsequently transferred the school to Liskeard and in 1785 she again assured parents and guardians that "unremitting attention" would be paid "to discharge the great duties and trust reposed in her". "Music, dancing and writing masters attend regularly". However, not long after she had a problem with "some few individuals, to serve their own private purposes" cruelly spreading a report that the school was "broke up", "at a time when nine boarders were just about to come to the school". She went on, "How callous must that heart be to every feeling of humanity, to endeavour to take the bread of a widow who has long been struggling under great misfortunes, and who has used every exertion to get a livelihood for herself and four innocent orphan girls". She had just recruited an accomplished teacher who had come down from one of the most genteel schools in London, "complete in the English and French languages and all kinds of needlework". She expressed her commitment to her charges in the future. Dancing, music and writing masters attended as heretofore. Board was then £12.12s per term. In January 1786 in addition to the other facilities of her school she advertised that they taught "fillagree, sheuil, embroidery, tambour, gold and silver, dresden and plain work". She stressed "There is no other lady's school in Liskeard but Mrs. Northcote's".

As well as her troubled establishment Liskeard had a grammar school which advertised its vacation times at the end of 1785, four weeks at Christmas, a fortnight at Whitsun and the same at Bartholomew-tide. Earlier in the year the mayor and capital burgesses announced that on the retirement of Rev. John Lyne, late master of the school, they had appointed his son, Rev. Richard Lyne, as his successor. The latter had moved "into a larger house than where he formerly resided, in an airy and pleasant part of the town, and very well fitted up for the accommodation of Young Gentlemen". He, his wife and mother would be "carefully attending as well to the health and happiness of young gentlemen as to their mental improvements. And as the minds of young people are then most ready to imbibe liberal sentiments when they meet with liberal treatment, such treatment will always be exhibited as one part of the system of education adopted in Liskeard." In 1790 Rev. Lyne had to counter some scurrilous verses that were circulating. "Whereas an insolent and anonymous copy of verses, directed to Mr. Hawkey, was found on Castle Hill, in the borough of Liskeard, on Saturday the 5th of June instant: - Whoever will discover the author of the same , so that the offender may be ascertained, and the odium of such indecencies be attached to the guilty only, shall be entitled to receive the sum of Ten Pounds of the Rev. Richard Lyne, of the said borough".

In 1784 a master was required at Lostwithiel "to teach writing and arithmetick, in the room of Mr. Trenow... [He] had upwards of sixty scholars, including those from the grammar-school, which is in a very flourishing state, and consists at present of upwards of forty scholars". In July 1786 several of the gentlemen educated at the grammar school advertised that they planned to hold an annual meeting, the first to be held in September. In 1791 the anniversary was held on 28th September, a sermon being preached with divine service at 11.30 a.m. In May 1790 the writing school was advertising for "a master well qualified to teach writing, arithmetic and drawing. His character must be good, and his English pronunciation pure". Eventually, in November, the position was taken up by Richard Julian "late clerk to the Cornish Metal Company". There was no Bartholomew-tide vacation at the grammar school that year owing to the election of the county representatives in parliament, whose poll began on 2nd July. The school opened again after it on 19th July. In May 1787 the Miss Jameses, "late of Liskeard", announced that they were establishing a boarding school for young ladies in the town. It would have similar concerns and facilities as that of Mrs. Northcote. Maybe they were her rivals in Liskeard. In 1792 the school moved to the "Mansion House at Restormel Park, very near to Lostwithiel. The house is roomy, and the walks around it so well known that Miss James has but little occasion to say how eligible the situation is for the residence of Young Ladies, whose parents or guardians may be assured, that every attention will be paid to the morals and education of those entrusted to her care. Every new and elegant Fancy Work taught. Also geography, French, music, dancing, writing and arithmetic."

Bodmin grammar school reopened after the Christmas vacation on 17th January 1791. "Rev. M. Morgan will continue to pay the strictest attention both the morals and improvement of those who may be placed under his care and instruction. There are several respectable families in the town, with whom young gentlemen may be comfortably boarded; there are likewise a few vacancies in the house with the master."

On the death of Mr. Dale the school at Tywardreath closed but was reopened by Charles Sloggett on 29th July 1793 for both boarders and day scholars. "Those ladies and gentlemen who are pleased to place their children with him may depend on the greatest attention being paid to their morals, as well as to their instruction in reading, writing, arithmetic and accompts... Those young gentlemen that chuse to learn French will be waited on at the school by an eminent master of that language, who is a native of France. Geometry, navigation, &c. will also be taught at the school. Tywardreath is a small, healthy village, near the sea coast, about three miles from Fowey."

Pupils who had attended Tregony grammar school held their anniversary meeting on 18th September 1787. Divine service at 11 a.m. was followed by a sermon by Rev. Stephen Doble. The one at Probus advertised in 1782 for a schoolmaster who could teach writing, arithmetic etc. Salary was £16 a year and he would be obliged to take ten poor children. It was said "Probus is a healthy situation and in a mid-country, and there is a large school room lately fitted up in a very neat manner".

Truro school was well established by this time and the annual reunion of gentlemen educated there was held on 8th September 1785. After meeting at the school house at 10 a.m. they proceeded to St.Mary's church where Rev. Francis Jenkins preached a sermon which was followed by dinner at Blight's, the Red Lion. At the reunion held on 18th September 1787, "some exercises" were performed by the young gentlemen in the morning and medals were distributed. This was followed by a sermon in the church, dinner at the Red Lion at 2 p.m. At an assembly in the evening the new room was opened. Similar proceedings were reported in 1789, 1792 and 1793. Writing schools established in the town which were supported by the mayor and corporation received criticism in 1785 and in December the town clerk saw fit to insert a notice in the paper that "they will make it their care to remove as far as it is in their power all just cause of complaint in future". A new school had then been opened "under their more immediate patronage" by William Petherick "whom they believe to be very well qualified for the employment he has undertaken". To help him he had a "proper assistant" and in the summer was opening an evening school for drawing. William Petherick retired after nearly seven years in 1791, having run the school "with general approbation" and was succeeded by Samuel Lambrick who in November advertised for an assistant "who can write a good hand, and understands common arithmetic".

In March 1790 Johanna Furly announced that she had established a school for young ladies at Penryn. "Her utmost attention will be paid to the morals, health and happiness of the young ladies whom she may have the honour to have under her care. The house she has taken, is indeed advantageously situated for the purpose, being on an eminence, and at a small distance from the town, with a pleasant green in front for the ladies to have proper exercise and amusement in". The school at Falmouth which William Borlase's grand-daughter attended when Mrs. Winchester had charge of it was that year taken over by Miss Hicks who advertised its facilities in April.

At Falmouth in 1784 J.Tolson continued "to instruct youth in every branch of learning to qualify them for business, also navigation in all its parts, with the use of the solar tables for the latitude by double altitudes, likewise lunar observations for ascertaining the longitude by a much easier and more concise method than any yet published. N.B. Three or four young gentlemen may be accommodated with board and lodging in the family". In 1793 a school opened at Falmouth "for the reception of young gentlemen from the age of five to twelve years of age. They are genteelly boarded, their morals taken care of, and every attention paid to their learning and health. The French language grammatically taught and spoken in the school, the Latin, and every useful branch of learning that is required, on very reasonable terms."

Helston grammar school's reunion was held at the Angel Inn on 23rd September 1789. Proceedings began at 10 a.m. when gentlemen educated at the school went to the church to hear a sermon. An assembly was held in the evening. In 1793 the anniversary was held on 18th September when after meeting at the Angel at 11 a.m. they proceeded to the church for a sermon by the master of the school, Rev. William Otter. Dinner was served at 3 p.m.

ANNUITANT SOCIETIES

For widows self-help organisations were established to provide them with security in their old age. A meeting was held at the house of Mrs. Mary Lanyon at Fowey on Monday 7th October 1782 at 4 p.m. to consider the plan to establish an Annuitant Society for the benefit of widows in the town. That at Launceston was already established in 1783 and their meeting was held at the King's Arms on Tuesday 24th June commencing at 11 a.m. There were about 20 vacancies. Dinner was served at 2 p.m. In 1790 their meeting was on the 30th June, starting at 10 a.m. The secretary, C. Lethbridge had "several sums of money ready to be advanced on freehold securities", suggesting that the societies loaned money locally on interest.

The meeting of the society at Falmouth was held on the last Tuesday of the month from February 1784 between 10 and noon until it was full. Age limit was 45. The annual meeting of the society at Liskeard, founded in 1784, was held on Tuesday 3rd January 1786 at the King's Arms. There were 12 vacancies in a membership of 100 and "£500 stock hath already been purchased for the use of the society, which being formed on the most approved plan, bids fair to be one of the most eligible and permanent of the kind". Dinner was served at 2 p.m. In 1788 the annual meeting was held on Tuesday 8th January at the same house, Mr. Webb's, the King's Arms. The fifth year's subscriptions of the first members was then completed and the signatures of members appended to articles agreed at the previous year's meeting. In 1789 it was held on Tuesday 5th January. People wanting to join should attend between 10 a.m. and 12 noon. Those unable to come should send the names and ages of their wives. Dinner was at 2 p.m.

In 1786 a society was formed at Tregony on the plan established at Padstow, the outlines of which were - "Every person who is admitted a member pays two guineas at the time of his admission, and the like sum annually afterwards. The widow of every member who shall die after he has paid four year's subscription (exclusive of his admission fine) will receive an annuity of £20". The first meeting of the society was held on 27th November at 1 p.m. when all "whose health, character, and conduct" rendered them eligible and who were under 45 were asked to attend. Meetings were held on the first Monday of February, March and April at the inn of Mr. Charles Harper to admit members. They would pay their subscriptions, attend divine service and dine at 1 p.m. The rules of the society were printed. At the meeting in 1788 held in the town hall on Tuesday 6th May at 10 a.m. it was stressed that "every person who wishes to be admitted a member will be expected to produce a certificate of his health, age, and (if married) the age of his wife, agreeable to the rules". Padstow's society held its general meeting on Tuesday 26th June 1792 at the George Inn. "There being a few vacancies, any person desirous of becoming a member of the said society, by applying either personally, or by his friend... will be admitted, provided he is found eligible by the rules of the said society".

The society at St.Austell had its annual meeting at the house of Thomas Tallack, innkeeper on Monday 31st March 1788 "for receiving the several annual subscriptions, admitting new members, and transacting the necessary business of the society". The meeting began at 10 a.m. and dinner was on the table at 1 p.m. "precisely". There were said to be a few vacancies in the society at Helston in 1790. Their meeting was held on 28th June, starting at 10 a.m. People wishing to become members should send their names to the secretary, T.Daniel. Dinner at 2 p.m. The new society at Truro held a meeting at the Red Lion on Monday 30th January 1792 at 11 a.m. "to transact the quarterly business &c. when those who have already given their names as candidates, and others who wish to become members, are requested to attend." In 1793 a meeting was held on Monday 29th April at 10 a.m. when members paid their subscriptions. "They are likewise to take notice, that all who have not produced certificates of their own and wives (if married), 'tis expected they will bring them on that day. Any who have already given, or may be desirous of giving in their names, as Candidates, to fill up the few remaining vacancies, are also requested to attend".

THE CHURCH

The role of the church continued to be a major one in people's lives, with births, marriages, deaths being commemorated within their purlieu. Much of the pastoral work was carried out by curates. "About a fortnight since [in July 1789] died, at St.Agnes, near Truro, the Rev. Mr. Harpur, who had been, for many years, curate of the parish, and lived very generally respected and esteemed in it. With a few frailties (and who is there without them?), he possessed many excellent qualities. He was liberal, humane and charitable. He discharged the duties of his function as a clergyman with attention and punctuality; and employed his abilities, as extensively as was in his power, to do good to his parishioners, and to all men. His exertions to promote a Sunday School in the parish, in conjunction with several benevolent neighbouring gentlemen, and the ultimate establishment of so excellent an institution will perpetuate his generosity and goodness of heart to future generations. Mr. Harpur's death was occasioned by his being thrown out of a one horse chaise, in consequence of which he received a bad fracture in his skull, and died the second day after the accident."

Some persons are known to have been conscientious, serving their cures responsibly and diligently. Many lived in some style. Rev. Richard Milles of Kenwyn was letting out Mylor vicarage in 1786. "The house is calculated for a small family, and consists of two parlours, kitchen, back-kitchen, and other convenient offices on the ground floor; with five separate bed-chambers, and one dressing-room on the second floor; stabling for five horses, with chaise-house, linhays, &c. its vicinity to the sea and the church, extensive command of water and of the beautiful country around, together with the salubrity of the air, convenience of markets, and cheapness of provisions, make it one of the most eligible retirements in the western kingdom. The garden is beautifully situate; and in high order, full of flowers and vegetables, and cropped with the choicest fruit-trees".

As well as their glebes parish clergy were supported by tithes on corn and hay (the great tithes) and on other lesser products, apples, honey, pigs, calves, lambs etc. Often tithes were "farmed", that is, rented, by an individual who collected the produce and paid their holder a lump sum. On 27th July 1786 a public survey was held at 6 p.m. at the house of James Gibson in St.Clement's street, near Truro for letting the great tithes of the parish of St.Clements. On 20th August a similar "survey" was held at the New Inn, Saltash for letting for seven years the great and small tithes of the parish of Landulph. To tempt potential farmers the advertisement went on - "the parish of Landulph is adjoining the river Tamar, and navigable from thence to Plymouth Dock, about seven miles, which renders it very convenient for the sale of all sorts of grain".

The rectories of parishes and rights of presentation were held in private ownership like other property. In December 1791 there was offered for sale "the next presentation and the perpetual right of every third turn of presenting to the rectory of St.Pinnock, Cornwall, worth at least £150 per annum. The situation is convenient and desirable, the living well conditioned, and hath a good glebe and parsonage house. The price paid and any further particulars may be had by application, either personally or by letter, to Mr. Henry Bate, the proprietor, of St.Cleer, Liskeard. N.B. If the above is not disposed of by private contract, before the last day of January 1792, of which notice will be given in this paper, a publick survey will held for it at the King's Arms, in Liskeard, on Wednesday the 1st of February, at two o'clock of the said day."

ECCLESIASTICAL COURTS

Ecclesiastical courts dealt with a whole range of matters, the proving of wills being one of the most important, marital matters, bastardy, sacrilegious behaviour etc. Cornwall was then within the diocese of Exeter and the chief cleric in the land was the archdeacon who held regular courts. In 1785 visitation courts were held on Tuesday 3rd May at Launceston, 4th May at Liskeard, 6th at Bodmin, Tuesday 10th at Truro, 12th at

Penzance and 14th Helston. "Where all persons having any wills to prove, or administrations to take, or any other business to do relative to the said court, may attend and have the same done." They were held at the same places on similar dates in 1786, 1788 and 1791.

DEBTS OWING

There were regular notices in the paper regarding those had claims on people's estates. They were to send in details to the executors or attorneys and if they owed money to the deceased they were to pay it by a certain date. Obviously this was a matter that particularly involved business people. This instance in 1784 - "All persons having any demands on the effects of William Petherick, watchmaker, late of St.Austell, deceased, are desired to send an account speedily to his widow or executrix or to Charles Rashleigh, attorney at law, at St.Austell. All indebted to her to pay the same forthwith." Others noted were Peter Garland of Illogan, shopkeeper, in 1783, Charles Jenkyn, late master of the brigantine Resolution of Padstow, John Williams of St.Austell, shopkeeper, in 1784, John Bennett, late of Gwinear, clerk, James Hearn of Padstow, sergemaker, in 1785, John Harvey, late of Liskeard, attorney at law in 1791, Joseph Langman of Calstock, victualler, and Richard Colmer of Millbrook, ropemaker, in 1792.

MARITAL PROBLEMS

Marital problems occasionally surfaced in the paper. In 1784 William Williams, of Helston, maltster, separated from his wife Mary, having previously made provision for her support and maintenance. In July he advertised that he would not pay any debt she contracted and that people should not give her credit on his account. John Richards of Kenwyn put in a notice in the following year regarding his wife. "For her misconduct towards me her said husband, [she] had rendered herself totally unworthy of the least respect from me: This is to caution the public not to credit her on my account, as I will not pay any debts she may contract from the day of notice, as witness my hand this 16th June 1785." In October 1786 Catherine, the wife of Abraham Cogar of St.Ives eloped from him and he put in an advertisement cautioning people not to trust her and that he would not pay debts contracted by her. In January 1787, William Webb of Gulval parish, ran away "leaving behind him a poor distressed wife with two daughters. He is a short thick man, with blue eyes, long strait hair, about fifty years of age, and by trade a pipe-maker. Was accompanied by one Ann French, a girl about twenty years of age, who passes for his wife, is pregnant by him, and supposed to be near the time of her delivery. It is hoped that no person will give them any countenance or protection, but that they may meet the fate such rogues and vagabonds deserve. N.B. The said Ann French was last year discharged from the bridewell at Bodmin."

Town. Haven & Castle of Fowey, Cornwall. Pl. 2.

Publish'd Dec. 14. 1785. by J. Hooper.

A Penzance man left his wife in 1789 - "Whereas Robert Matthews... by trade a miller, and sometimes a butcher, went off the day after Christmas-day last, with his servant maid; and left his wife (a prudent careful woman) and three children, and she just ready to have a fourth; and carried off with him several sums of money, which ought to be paid for the rent of his mills, land, &c. This is to caution all clergymen not to marry him, and the public not to trust him. N.B. The said Robert Matthews is a thin man, of a pale complexion, about 5 feet 9 inches high, wore his own dark brown hair, had on a dark green coast, and a whiteish drab surtout coat. The wench he went off with is near his height, of a reddish complexion, black hair, and had on a red and white striped cotton gown." The following year Mary Pomery left her husband, William, saddler and bookbinder, of Launceston. She went off "with determination never to return to him again". In his notice William said that he would "not discharge any debts contracted by her".

DEFAMATION OF CHARACTER

The schoolmistress of Liskeard, Mrs. Northcote complained of someone spreading rumours about her school. The newspaper was used by other individuals to counter such stories and defamations of character, etc. An advertisement appeared in the paper on 7th April 1783 for selling the entire stock in trade of Richard Gray in Redruth on 21st April. Mr. Gray subsequently put in a notice informing the public that it was "the work of some ill designing persons; and whoever will give information who the person or persons is or are, shall, on conviction of them, receive of Richard Gray a reward of ten guineas. N.B. My trade will be continued as usual." Thomas Dickinson of Kenwyn, paper-maker, being at Padstow, had a quantity of paper taken out of his cart and carried away in February 1784. Richard Elliott of Padstow was accused of taking the paper. Thomas Dickinson later put in a notice to inform the public in general, "in vindication of Richard Elliott's character, that there appeared, on enquiry into the matter, no intention of fraud in the said Richard's Elliott's behaviour."

On 24th April the same year William Rawling of Penryn, carpenter, apologised for having "violently assaulted and cruelly beaten Mr. John Dixon, of the said place, grocer, before a great number of spectators, without any reason or provocation whatever." He begged Mr. Dixon not to commence a prosecution against him for the assault, "as I hope this public concession will deter him therefrom." Two years later, on Monday 27th February, "Nathaniel Phillips, a young man about the age of 16, an indentured apprentice to Benjamin Moon, of this borough, cordwainer, deliberately put an end to his existence by hanging himself. As it has since been wickedly and maliciously reported, that the ill-treatment the apprentice had received from his master was the cause of his committing that desperate act: The underwritten do, for the satisfaction of the said Benjamin Moon and his friends, declare that nothing tending to injure the said Benjamin's character was advanced by either of the witnesses examined at the inquest.

John Thomas, mayor and coroner. Samuel Thomas, foreman. William Jackson, churchwarden. the above-named Benjamin Moon gives this public notice, that if any person or persons shall or do want only traduce his character respecting the above melancholy deed, they shall be prosecuted as the law directs."

The same year Richard Harris of Pulherna in St.Keverne, yeoman, on the 9th September, accused Francis Johns of St.Keverne, yeoman, of being a rogue and a thief, and that he had stolen the money of Michael Amerson. Johns caused a prosecution to be commenced against him and Harris put in a notice declaring that he did not know "the said accusation to be true, nor had proper foundation for so saying, but the same was done in liquor; in consideration of which, and my paying the costs and charges, and acknowledging my fault by signing this advertisement, the said Francis John has consented to stay the said suit."

In May 1788 Lewis Sanders acknowledged that he had "grossly insulted, and publickly made use of very foul language towards Mr. Robert Donnall, of Penryn, tending to asperse the character and reputation of Mr. Donnall, amongst other things charging him with perjury, for which he has very justly threatened to commence a prosecution". He consented to put a stop thereto on his publicly acknowledging his fault. Sanders declared that he had "not the slightest reason to doubt the integrity or to believe he ever was, or would be, guilty of what [he] laid to his charge, and [was] sorry to have made use of such unwarrantable and abusive language towards him."

An advertisement appeared in the Sherborne Mercury of Monday the 19th October 1789 offering a reward of ten guineas for a letter addressed to a person of consequence, supposed to be lost out of the pocket of W. Hichens of Newlyn between Mr. Stephen Luke's and his house. Later in the month Mr. Hichens put in a notice assuring the public that such advertisement was inserted without his knowledge or approbation "and that the matter contained in it is entirely without foundation, and calculated for no other purpose than to support a grosser imposition since practised on the public in this neighbourhood."

Owing to "false and malicious suggestions of some evil minded persons" a prosecution was instituted against Richard Ferris, of St.Clement Street, near Truro in 1790. He put a notice in the paper in August informing the public that "he alone intends to carry on the tanning business; that the woolstapling and fellmongering business will also, as before, be continued by the said Richard and John Ferris, under the firm of Richard Ferris and Son". John Ferris informed his friends and customers that in order to assist his father who is infirm he had quitted the trades of currier and leather cutter in favour of his brother William. John Ferris was involved in another case a few years later. "Whereas a scandalous report has been brought out and propagated by some evil designing person or persons, that Mr. Richard Hayes, of the parish of Gerrans... should have thrown a large quantity of water on some wool he lately sold to Mr. John Ferris... in order to defraud..." the latter put in a notice in the paper on 5th January 1793 stating that "for several years last past [he had] bought wool of Mr. Richard Hayes... and always found him to act as a very honest man; that I bought his last two years' wool, and some little time since weighed it off; and that I do verily believe that the said Mr. Hayes never put or suffered to be put any water into the said wool, nor did anything thereby to injure the same". His testimony was backed up by two men of Gerrans, Joseph Hichens and John Rowe, who both signed their statements with a cross.

At St. Ewe in 1791 Ann Pearce acknowledged that she had "wantonly and maliciously endeavoured to defame the character of Ann Searle of Probus" for which proceedings had justly been commenced against her. By inserting a notice in the paper, begging her pardon, promising not to be guilty of the same in future and paying the costs, Ann Searle had dropped the prosecution. Like several others in the paper she signed her name with a cross. The same year three sailors were using a forged pass with the name of Edward Giddy J.P. and other gentlemen on it. The men were then thought to be in south Devon or Dorset. People were alerted that if the pass was produced, they should secure the same, apprehend the sailors and take them before a magistrate so that they could be dealt with according to the law. In Penryn a publication by a businessman in the town, Benjamin Heame, offended Richard Oates in 1791. A notice was put in the paper on his behalf - "it is enough at present to say, that proper directions have been given to the solicitors concerned. The attempts of Mr. Oates's enemies to accomplish his ruin will certainly recoil on themselves. The public are desired to withhold their judgement for a short period, when the characters of both Mr. Oates and Mr. Heame will be brought forward, and the transactions of each, as men of business, made known. The solicitors of Mr. Oates have been directed, without regard to expence, to prosecute all persons, who shall, by improper means, dare to injure his reputation."

Richard Treneer of Gluvias, a butcher, had to make an apology the following year - "Whereas I... have lately propagated a false report, tending to injure and reflect on the character of William Thomas, of Tregerland, within the parish of St.Just in Roseland... with his dealers, as a grazier, for which a prosecution has been commenced against me". Thomas stayed his proceedings and Treneer declared that he "had no reason whatever for affecting such a falsehood, and do believe that the said William Thomas was not, nor could be guilty of such an act as was laid to his charge." In March 1793 Richard Straight had printed a counter to an accusation against him - "Whereas a report has lately been spread, that I should have sent my servant to Truro market with oats of two different qualities in one sack, in order to deceive the public, I take this method to inform all those that may have heard such report, that is without the least foundation; and I hereby offer a handsome reward to any person or persons who will discover the author or authors of the aforesaid report, being fully determined to prosecute him or them with the utmost rigour of the law".

VANDALISM

Vandalism also was problem at this time. "Whereas certain ill-designed people did, on Sunday night, October 26th 1783, pull down and destroy many pales of a plantation in Pencarroe Park, and otherwise damaged a gate of the park: This to give notice, that any person giving such intelligence, as that the said offences shall be convicted, shall receive Fifty Guineas reward. Application to be made to Mr. William Symons, of St.Minver, or Mr. Samuel Hext, in Bodmin. Pencarrow." In the section on inland transport it was noticed how damage was done to Grampound bridge in 1789. The situation was no doubt aggravated by the depression in the mines and the example of revolutionary conditions across the channel. At St.Agnes in 1791 "some malicious person or persons have within nine months last, as it is supposed set fire to the dwelling-houses of John Paul of Trevisick, in the said parish, at three different times, whereby not only the dwelling-houses, but also twenty-five load of wheat, seven load of barley, and five load of hay, were entirely destroyed, to the damage of the said John Paul, at least £300". At their meeting on Easter Monday the parishioners of the parish at their public vestry offered a reward of twenty guineas to any person or persons who could prove who committed "this atrocious act". The same amount would go any who gave evidence to convict the offenders. The parishioners recommended Mr. Paul "as a public object of charity. Subscriptions to be received at the two Banks in Truro, the Bank at Falmouth, and the Churchwardens and Overseers of this parish".

ASSIZES

When offenders were caught they were dealt with by J.P.s, local courts and the assizes held at this time twice a year, at Launceston in the spring and Bodmin in August. In March 1786 D.Douglas Esq. was found guilty of the manslaughter of Mr. Walton and imprisoned for one year. Clearly there must have been mitigating circumstances. At the same time three men were capitally convicted of sheep stealing. Three others including a woman were reprieved from execution for the offence. Two other women, for stealing clothes and fleeces of wool respectively, were sentenced to be whipped and imprisoned for one year; John Knight, alias Goodman, convicted of manslaughter was to be burnt in the hand and imprisoned for one year; another man for the same offence was fined 1s and imprisoned for one year and the same punishment was given to a man for stealing beef. Thirteen were convicted and the same number acquitted.

Not long after the assizes, in early April two farmers going from Penryn to Falmouth at night were robbed of their watches and 15s in silver. The robbers were found to be two men from H.M.S. Fairy in Falmouth port. They appeared at the assizes at Bodmin in August and were capitally convicted as was William Conolly who about to be transported had escaped from Bodmin gaol. They appear, however, to have been reprieved as were two men who stole sheep and a horse. Seven years transportation was the punishment of William Roberts who stole yarn from a man at Launceston and Walter Stapleton who stole two yards of corduroy. At the assizes an address was made to the king congratulating him on his recent escape from assassination. The Grand Jury also requested that prisoners at Bodmin and the hulk at Plymouth should be sent abroad - presumably there was a delay in carrying out their sentence of transportation.

The assizes began at 8 a.m. on Monday 26th March 1787 in the assize hall at Launceston. James Elliott, aged 18, was capitally convicted for robbing the mail and sentenced to be hung in chains but on account of his having revealed the place where the mail bag with the letters was, namely, in a tin shaft in the parish of Padstow, that part of the sentence which related to his being hung in chains was remitted. Several others were capitally convicted for robbery but only John Gould who broke into the house of Thomas Warne at Budock was executed. Seven years transportation was the punishment of Richard Skinner who stole from the warehouses of Niels Falck, Charles George who took three to four cwt. of black tin from Dawran stamps and Michael Thomas who stole a quantity of potatoes from a dwelling house in Stithians. Two charged with murder were acquitted as were 11 others for lesser offences. Some for pretty offences were whipped.

At the August assizes three were capitally convicted - James Barnicoat alias Lavers for "breaking open" the house of Thomas Ivy of Camborne and stealing £80, William Marks for stealing a silver watch from Mary Hicks and William Congdon for stealing a silver watch and chain from Francis Kelly of Rame. Marks was reprieved but the others were executed. Richard Reynolds alias Runnalls for breaking open the house of Francis Hutton and stealing part of a "potatoe pasty", Benjamin Dunstone and William Bolithoe for assaulting and beating William Singleton on the highway and robbing him of a box containing half-pence to the value of 5s and a French half-crown were to be transported for seven years. William Polglase and Thomas Thomas who had obtained certain goods from Mr. Russell of Dungarvon in the county of Waterford, Ireland were to be removed to Ireland. One was ordered to be whipped and four acquitted. William Daw charged with assaulting and obstructing Christopher Childs, excise officer, in the execution of his duty was ordered to remain in confinement.

A new goal was built at Bodmin and in May 1789 tenders were invited for the construction of an attic storey in the sheriff's ward. At the assizes at Bodmin in August following only two prisoners were tried "a circumstance highly honourable to the county", one of whom was capitally convicted, John Burris, for stealing two silver table and four silver tea spoons out of the house of Samuel Skinnard - "he was reprieved before the judges left town" - and James Ball for manslaughter in killing John Clark. The latter was imprisoned for six months. No bill was found against John Treviling, charged with burglary. Also at this assizes Justice Buller gave a decision regarding the import of spirits and teas from France and Guernsey "which must materially affect the smuggling business in this county". The plaintiff's counsel was allowed to seek the opinion of the court of King's Bench. A case was brought by William Fowler, attorney, against Sir William Molesworth, J.P. for an assault and false imprisonment but a witness called on behalf of the plaintiff did not appear occasioning general laughter in the court. When the witness did appear the judge would not permit the matter to be tried until the next morning. After the grand jury was dismissed it was resolved by a majority of the gentlemen who dined with the sheriff that an address should be presented to King George on his visit to Plymouth the following Friday.

A case was reported in the Sherborne Mercury shortly after where a woman at Falmouth gave birth to a "bastard child" and concealed it. Elizabeth Madsen was the wife of Christian, a mariner, who had been absent from the town for several years. She refused at first to admit that she had been pregnant but later said she had miscarried. Suspicions having been aroused a warrant was secured from a J.P. for her to be examined by a midwife. Information was given to the parish officers that there was in her apartment a small vault for the purpose of secreting prohibited goods, and they searched the same and found the body of a dead female child. Having been informed of the discovery she confessed that she had been delivered of the baby on the 4th September and that immediately had thrust it into a pair of old breeches, wrapped it up in her petticoat and buried it in the vault. She would not say if the baby had been born alive. Its body was in so putrid a state that it could not be examined as to whether there were any marks on violence on it. The coroner's inquest found that she was guilty of murder and she was sent to goal.

In December Christopher Hawkins committed to Bodmin goal Henry Whitty, alias Wilson, of about 40, and John Harvey about 32, who were charged with having stolen a women's apparel, a satin cloak, a shift, two petticoats, a handkerchief, a gown and a satin work bag and divers other articles which had been found on them. A notice was put in the paper asking people whose possessions these were to apply to Hawkins. Around the same time three young men had deserted from his Majesty's 74th Regiment of Foot at Bodmin, John Hawkey, born in St.Columb, William Crawl or Crowll born in St.Ewe, William Powell from St. Ervan. Whoever would lodge the men in any of his Majesty's gaols would receive £1. Powell and Crowll were thought to be about Plymouth Dock and "are notorious poachers and bastard getters". In January 1790 a young man called Pascoe was charged with setting fire to a dwelling house at Flushing near Falmouth. Smoke issuing from an apartment in the house "occasioned by fire having been put amongst some furze" happily led to its discovery before any mischief was done. Pascoe was committed to goal.

At the assizes in March at Launceston 15 prisoners were tried of whom two were capitally convicted - Joseph Bullock, aged 25, convicted of stealing a guinea and some sugar from the house of Nathaniel Lang and Zimram Uram, aged 21, for stealing two guineas of Philip Body. Both were reprieved. Thomas Gardner for stealing a pair of blankets etc. from T.Thorp Fowkes Esq. was transported for seven years. Thomas Crocker for manslaughter in killing John Nicholls was fined 1s and discharged. Benjamin Pascoe, aged 20, on suspicion of setting a room on fire in the house of William Hillman in Flushing was admitted to bail until the next assizes. Elizabeth Madson, aged 53, for murdering her bastard child, Henry Witty, alias Wilson, John Harvey and Jane Witty for stealing a quantity of goods and wearing apparel, James Paul for stealing sundry articles, John and Grace Rusden for receiving stolen goods from James Paul, and William Strongman indicted for an attempt to commit an unnatural crime, were acquitted.

At the assizes at Bodmin in August three were capitally convicted, Thomas James and Thomas Mills for a burglary in the house of Rev. Coppelstone Radcliffe and stealing a silver tea-kettle and sundry other articles of plate, John Barberry for burglariously stealing out of the house of Malachi Bice four silver spoons and one pair of shoes. James was left for execution but Mills and Barberry were reprieved. Rebecca Trennery for stealing articles of wearing apparel, the property of Cadelia Jenkins, was imprisoned for six months and fined one shilling. No bills were found in the cases of Jenefrid Jenkins, charged with two felonies, Gilbert Barkle, charged with stealing a pair of shoes. Arthur Southey charged with killing a sheep and three others were acquitted. An attorney brought a case against a Mr. Fowler for money expended on behalf of the defendant's wife. It appeared Mr. Fowler had married a lady of Bristol, his third wife, about four years before, with a fortune of £4,000. He brought her to his seat near Bodmin but mistreated her and eventually she left him in October 1788, went to a magistrate and exhibited articles against him. He was taken into custody and given bail and subsequently appeared at two quarter sessions and sued in the ecclesiastical court for a divorce. "After a trial of several hours, in which many laughable incidents occurred, the plaintiff obtained a verdict for £22 to the satisfaction of a crowded court".

At the assizes at Bodmin in August 1791 three were capitally convicted - William Willoughby and John Taylor for murdering James James and William Moyle for killing a mare the property of Daniel Bartlett. Willoughby and Taylor were two soldiers of the 33rd regiment quartered at Helston. James was a publican. The couple had gone to his house at about midnight one night and demanded some liquor but were refused. They went away but soon afterwards returned and made the same request in a peremptory manner. The landlord still refusing one or them laid hold of him in a scuffle having reached the fore-door Willoughby struck James on the head with his bayonet which fractured his skull and he died two days after. They were executed on the 2nd September. Moyle was a smuggler and Bartlett an excise officer. It appeared that the prisoner committed this offence in revenge against the officer who had a little before seized some smuggled goods belonging to him. Presumably he too was executed though the report does not say so. Also at the assizes John Hancock was convicted of stealing two watches and was fined 6d and imprisoned for six months, Benjamin Dale was convicted of an attempt to steal fowls and was fined 6d and imprisoned for one year. Robert Hatton, William Walters, and John Charles who were charged with assaulting and obstructing John Hickman, Samuel Maunders and Jonathan Bustle, officers of the customs, in the execution of their duty on 11th April 1791 were committed to Dorchester gaol. Judge Buller was in sole charge of proceedings, Lord Loughborough not coming into Cornwall.

In December 1791 Nathaniel Lawrence, under sentence of transportation, escaped from Launceston gaol. About 24 years of age, five foot four inches high, fair complexion, with dark brown short hair he was wearing a white callimanco coat and breeches, velveret red and white waistcoat, the red almost washed out, black yarn stockings and old canvas shirt. Whoever would apprehend him and lodge him in one of

Engrav'd by W. Watkins from a drawing by J. Britton for the Beauties of England & Wales.

PROBUS TOWER,
Cornwall.

London, Published by Vernon & Hood, Poultry, June 1 1805.

his Majesty's gaols would receive three guineas over and above that allowed by act of parliament. Not long after a man suspected of being concerned in the robbery of mail between Warrington and Manchester and the murder of the post-boy was on the run in Cornwall. He had been living for a time in Exeter under the name of Whiteman but suspicions having been aroused he was followed into Cornwall and at Bodmin was arrested by Thomas Wood of Exeter. When he was put into fetters in Launceston gaol he burst into tears. He said he had always been an unfortunate man, that he should soon be at large and hoped the public would know, in the course of a week, who was the mail robber.

At the assizes at Bodmin in August 1792 three were capitally convicted but afterwards reprieved - William Brawn and William Williams for a highway robbery on Nicholas May and Peter Retallo for a burglary. William Hodge, charged with being concerned in robbing Nicholas May, was admitted King's evidence. George Belton, convicted of stealing three horses, the property of Arthur Hoskin was transported for seven years. Thomas Woolcok was found guilty of having assaulted Richard Corfield, an excise officer, in the execution of his office, and Roger Couch, convicted of stealing various articles of wearing apparel, the property of Stephen Gilbert, was imprisoned for six months. Five were acquitted.

In March 1793 at Launceston William Trevervas was executed at St.Stephen's near Launceston for robbing and murdering Martha Blewett. Before his execution he confessed and said that he divided the money which he took from the deceased, £29, between a woman, to whom he was soon to be married, his father and sister. Others were capitally convicted but afterwards reprieved. Ann Richards, aged 19, for a burglary in the dwelling-house of Abraham Dowah, Martin Cunnow, for robbing and beating Elizabeth Hancock on the highway and William Robins for stealing two sheep, the property of Henry Benallie of Creed. There were only six prisoners tried at the assizes at Bodmin in August and five were acquitted. Thomas Brown Holmes was found guilty of a fraud in that he paid a counterfeit dollar to one Mary Woolcock. In a case before a special jury the mayor and burgesses of Saltash sued the master of a ship for loading dues in the river Tamar. After a trial of five hours the defendant, Thomas Galilee, won the case.

ELECTIONS

Elections and parliamentary news in the paper. Following the elevation of Edward Eliot to the Upper House as Lord Eliot, Baron St.Germans in 1784 a meeting of the gentlemen, clergy and freeholders was called to consider a successor. This signed by J. St.Aubyn, Francis Bassett, John Morshead, F.Lemon Rogers, William Praed, N. Donnithorne, W. Molesworth on 26th January 1784 The last named, Sir William Molesworth of Pencarrow, was duly elected. At the parliamentary election in April W.A.Spencer Boscawen and William McCarmick thanked the burgesses of Truro for electing them to be their members of parliament. "It shall be the study of our lives to merit the confidence you have been pleased to repose in us, by a constant attendance on our duty in Parliament, by an invariable attention to the commercial interests of our constituents, and by a zealous attachment to the true principles of the constitution".

John St.Aubyn of Clowance put in a notice in September 1789 thanking people for their support at the county meeting. "The decided manner in which you have declared your disapprobation of the conduct of my competitor in his unprecedented canvas, must surely induce him to withdraw his pretensions, and convince him that this county is still determined to support its independence". The election on 2nd July 1790 was a hard fought one. On 16th June Francis Gregor of Restormel Park inserted the following notice in the Sherborne Mercury - "I have met with such encouragement in my canvas of the county, as to afford the most sanguine hopes that I shall obtain the honour of being appointed to represent it by a considerable majority of the freeholders, whose sense I am fully determined to take, by abiding the event of a poll. The assurances of perfect independence, and of zeal for the interests of this county, and of the kingdom at large, which I formerly gave, I can with the greatest sincerity repeat." At the election he and the long-standing M.P. Sir William Lemon triumphed.

The excitement and interest the election generated is evident from other notices in the paper. Under "Horse Found at Bodmin" there was a report - "The following horse was left at Bodmin during the late election for Cornwall:- A DARK BAY NAG, about 14 hands high; black mane and tail (swish tail), white star in forehead; white stroke down his face, turning over the nearer nostril; unfound; saddle and bridle left with him. The owner may have the same by applying to Walter Spry, at the Star, Bodmin, and paying the charges". Also "Lost, out of a field at Lostwithiel, at the election, A LIGHT GREY GELDING, swish tail, the fore hoofs black, the hind ones white; has had two broken knees. Whoever will bring the said horse to T.Walker, Frankfort Place, Plymouth, shall receive Half a Guinea reward, and all expences". From Helston in November under "Cornwall Election" - "To prevent the several Persons who have demands on Sir John St.Aubyn from making applications which are both expensive and troublesome, they are hereby informed, that proper persons will attend at each town to liquidate and settle all Election Accounts between this time and the 25th day of December next".

LOST AND STOLEN

Items lost or stolen were advertised in the paper. At Tandean, Perran, near the foundation of Richard Share's house, 7 bars of long and 42 bars of short iron, were found and then held (1st October 1782) by Thomas Daniell at his plating forge house there. Owner could have same after paying cost of advert. Share's house was very near the forge and the iron was suitable for making fire engine boiler plates. In June 1785 there was found lying in the warehouse of Harris, Ellis and Co. at Carnsew, in the port of Hayle, one small parcel of goods, marked or directed to Messrs. Stephens and Roberts, Camborne. It had never been enquired for by any one. Any person who had a right or proper title to the same, could have it for paying the expence on it, otherwise it would be sold by public auction in the space of one month after the notice.

At the Michaelmas fair at Marazion on Saturday the 29th of September 1787 was lost a small pocket ledger, in which was a bill of exchange, value twenty-two pounds, drawn the 7th September 1787 by Mr. Geo. Semmons, of Tresamble, Gwennap, in Cornwall, in favour of Anthony Richards, No.170. The last indorser was Messrs. John Batten and Son, made payable to John Hosking, 29th September, 1787. Whoever found the book and would deliver it, with the bill to John Hosking, of Penzance, would receive of him five guineas reward. On Friday evening the 9th October 1789, between Bodmin and St.Columb, were lost two gold seals; one a red Cornelian, with the cyphers C.C and a spread eagle crest over the same; the other a white Cornelian, with a falcon engraved thereon. Whoever took them to Mr. Tippet, attorney, at Falmouth or Mr. Prater, attorney, St.Columb, would receive half a guinea reward. At Penzance William Thomas lost a silver watch on the night of 24th June 1791. It was attached to a silver chain and large seal. Watchmakers and pawnbrokers were desired to observe the maker's name, Lazarus Solomon of London, No.5180, with the day of the month in the dial-plate. It was believed the watch was lost near the quay and probably some seamen had picked it up. Any person on whom the watch was found after the advertisement would be prosecuted with the utmost severity.

Dogs were periodically lost and found. As well as those already mentioned there was the following. A remarkable fine large dog, supposed to be of the Newfoundland breed, had been found in Cornwall in January 1787 and it was then with a person who would willingly restore it to its owner. From the circumstances of its having tar about it, and (though fed) going every evening to one particular spot on the rocks under the cliffs, looking out to the sea, and moaning as if its master was there, gave cause to imagine it belonged to a captain of a vessel. For further information, people should apply to Messrs. Haydon and Son, booksellers, stationers and printers, Plymouth. Lost at Truro on 29th August 1787, a small yellow and white beagle bitch, about 14" high which answered to the name of Fairmaid. Any person bringing it to Mr. Rivers, innholder, in Truro, would receive half a guinea reward. Whoever detained her after the notice would be prosecuted.

Lost, supposed to be stolen, from the kennel at Gulval, near Penzance, in April 1789 a young fox-hound bitch, a year and half old, about 20 inches high, short rounded ears, hare pied, with yellowish spots, a remarkable fine back, stood very straight on her legs, and answered to the name of Coaxer. Whoever brought information of her to Mr. Pethick, or the huntsman at Gulval, so that she was recovered, should be handsomely rewarded for his trouble. Any person or persons concealing or detaining the bitch, after the public notice, would be prosecuted with the utmost severity. In October 1790 a lively young dog, liver-coloured and white, with a cross of the pointer in him, followed Mr. Trevenen, of Helston, from Hayle Copper House. Writing on the 18th the dog was still in his possession and would be delivered to the owner, on his paying the expence of advertising etc. Strayed from the town of Marazion on Monday, 17th September 1792 a strong, bony, liver coloured and white pointer dog about 10 months old which answered to the name of Sancho. Information to Capt. John James of Marazion or Mr. James Goff, stud groom at Clowance. One guinea reward and reasonable costs.

Undoubtedly some of the animals that went missing had been stolen. Horses were particularly vulnerable, four in 1783 alone. As well as that belonging to John Trevenen of Helston the following - "From Hingston Commons, near Callington on Thursday night 17th April, a sorrel saddle mare, about 13½ hands, five years old, has a full mane, lying on the further side, thick shouldered, and has several white spots, like two laits(?), on the ribs, on the near side, with a swish tail. When she stands in any house her near foot is generally forward. Whoever will give news of the mare to Edward Wilkey shall receive half a guinea reward, Callington, 19th April." "Stolen or strayed in the evening of 13th April out of a field belonging to John May of Trelask in Pelynt, a black mare, now eight years old, about 13½ hands high. Has a remarkable tight mouth, her mane hangs the farther side, and had when taken a short swish tail. Whoever informs John May or Samuel May, grocer, of East Looe, where the said mare is, so as she may be had again shall receive half a guinea reward but if found after this publication in any person's keeping, they will be prosecuted according to the law. Dated 3rd May." "St.Columb. Strayed or conveyed, last night (22nd August) a brown gelding, about 13½ hands high, eight years old, very thick mane, short back and well made. Whoever can give information thereof, so as the said gelding may be had again, to Mr. Catton of St.Columb, shall be rewarded by him (the owner)."

"Stolen or strayed, the 11th November, 1785, from Mr. Thomas Carbis, Back-yard, in Redruth, at the sign of the Queen's Head, a black gray nag, about 13 hands and a half high or thereabout: his mane parts on both sides of his neck, a thick shoulder, and a swish tail; had on a pack saddle, and is about four years old, coming five. Whoever will bring or send news of the said nag, to Mr. William Newton, at the Duke's Head, in Penzance, so that the right owner may have it again, shall receive half a guinea reward, and all reasonable charges paid. Dated 18th December, 1785." On the 22nd July 1786, a man naming himself Thomas Dale, travelling from Plymouth to the western part of Cornwall, came to the house of William Netherton, at the sign of the Jolly Sailor, in Lostwithiel, with "a dark grey mare, about fourteen hands high, and about five years old, with a large tail, something whiter than her body, never jointed, unless done since, with a white spot on the inside of her near hock, a little short the gamberl(?)" Dale exchanged the mare with Netherton for a dark bay gelding. On the night of 26th July the gelding was brought back and put into a field belonging to him and the mare taken away. Netherton put a notice in the Sherborne Mercury requesting information on the whereabouts of the mare. He would pay half a guinea reward.

On Wednesday night 25th October 1786, an iron grey mare, about 14 hands high, and 5 years old, used to labour was stolen out of the ground of Mr. White of Grampound. Whoever could give notice of the said mare to him so that she may be had again, would be paid all reasonable charges, and be rewarded for their trouble. On Friday the 2nd February 1787, from Perdreda, in the parish of St.German's, a short-set grey gelding, twelve or thirteen hands high, with a thick head, hollow eyes, about twelve years old was taken. William Rogers, of Perdreda offered half a guinea reward for its recovery. In February the following year a white nag pony, about 11 hands and a half high, goose mugg'd, a swish tail, the mane hanging on the off side was stolen or strayed from Clowance. It belonged to Mr. Samuel Pollard, of Newlyn, in the parish of Paul. Whoever found it and brought it to the hind at Clowance, Mr. Pollard, or Mr. Richard Scaddan, of Penzance, should be handsomely rewarded.

"Stolen or strayed, from the parish of St.Kew, on the night of the 10th of this September 1789, a strawberry mare, about 14 hands high, a short tail, a hog mane, a white spot in the forehead, some white under both fetterlocks of the hind feet, and some red spots in the saddle place; the property of George Tucker. Whoever will give notice of the said mare, to George Tucker, of St.Kew, so that she may be had again, shall receive half a guinea reward, and all reasonable expences paid." "Stolen or strayed from Bodrean, in the parish of St. Clements, in October 1789 a dark bay mare, about four years old and 14 hands high; turns in her fore feet very much, and jointed long, with a black list on her back." Whoever brought the mare or gave information to Mr. Andrew of St.Erme, so it was recovered should receive half a guinea reward, and all reasonable expences.

Stolen or strayed from Nelo, near Helston on 16th May 1791 a bright bay nag, about 13 hands high, three years old, never shod, jointed tail, rather long. Ten shillings for information to Jethro Hornblower, two guineas, if stolen, upon conviction. On 25th July the stables of John Coad of Helston were broken open and a dark bay mare stolen. The commissioners of the customs offered £10 for information about the offenders to be paid by Tremenheere Johns collector of the port. On 25th April 1793 a small bay nag pony with a slit in the near ear and a white saddle spot on the farther side was taken from William Hawken at Tremain in Pelynt. Half a guinea reward for information. Early July a dark bay mare pony was thought to have been ridden off from the King's Head premises, Truro. The pony was about nine years old, or may be more, between 12 and 13 hands high, short swish tail, strong made, a remarkable good trotter, very spirited and carried her head high, had a striped mark on her right side (which the saddle covered) and an inch or inch and half long, apparently scratched with a nail or a bullock's horn, and had not been trimmed for some time. News of the pony to Mr. Howard, King's Head or S.Plovis, Truro.

Cattle and sheep were also liable to theft. "Stolen or strayed from Brown Willy, in the parish of Simonward, some time in June last. Two brown two years old heifers, burnt in the near horn with the letters, J.E. and a hole in the near ears. If strayed, any person or persons giving news of the same, so that they may be had again, to Mr. Henry Hocken of the parish of Michaelstow or William Hocken of Trenarlett, in St.Tudy, shall receive a half guinea reward. If stolen, any person or persons giving information thereof, so as the offender or offenders may be brought to justice, shall, upon the conviction of the offender or offenders, receive five guineas reward, of the said Henry and William Hocken. Dated 20th October 1783". On December 12th 1787 five guineas reward was offered for information as to who stole two fat sheep off the estate of Selian Vean, in the parish of Sancreed, on the previous Friday last, about 11 o'clock at night. Two men were seen about that time riding out of the estate; one dressed in blue coat and breeches, with a poor hat, on a bay horse; the other a whitish frock, on a large grey horse, with something tied up in sheeting. Mr. Peter Ellis would give the reward when the offenders were brought to justice. "Supposed to be stolen from Trehannick in the parish of St.Teath, by Camelford, on Tuesday night 22nd September, 20 sheep marked with pitch in the further side thus with an N backwards, and the ear mark is topped on both ears, and slit in both stocks. Whoever can give information of the said sheep to Nicholas Male of St.Teath, so that the offender or offenders may be brought to justice, shall receive Five guineas reward. Dated St.Teath, October 13, 1789."

Stolen on the night of 21st April 1792 from Treveary in Probus two fat wether sheep the property of James Drew. Ten guineas reward offered for conviction of the thieves. From Tewkenbury Common in St.Ive about the latter end of January 1793 39 wether sheep disappeared, pitch-marked with J.E. on the near side behind the pin, redded on the further pin; ear mark, a top cut on the further ear, with a square halfpenny under, and a spade on the near ear. Information so that they may be had again to John Ellet would be rewarded with two guineas.

Advertised in the paper were other items that had been stolen. "Stolen out of the dwelling house of Mrs. Grace James of Lostwithiel in the night of 29th September a silver watch, maker's name, Robert Wood, London, No. 960. Whoever will discover the said watch and return it, Mrs James will pay all charges. If after this advertisement the watch should be discovered, the person on whom it is found may depend on being prosecuted as the law directs. Dated, 20th October 1783." "Whereas in the night of Thursday, the 12th February 1784, the house of Jonathon Nicholls, the Queen's Head Inn, Truro, was broken open by some person or persons yet undiscovered and from thence stole eleven silver spoons, seven of which were of one mould, with a flower or branch on the back of the bowl, and marked on the stem with the letters INM, the four others plain; also a money box belonging to a Friendly Society, was likewise carried off, out of which was taken nearly £11. If the above spoons should be offered for sale pray stop them, and any person giving information, so as he or they may be brought to justice, shall, on conviction, receive the sum of five guineas from me, J. Nicholls. 20th February 1784."

Henry Perry put a notice in the paper in January 1785 regarding Joseph Weals who robbed his house at Camborne of several articles - he may have been his apprentice. Perry offered five guineas reward to any person or persons who brought Weals to justice. He was "about five feet eleven inches high, red hair, of a fair complexion, and had on when he went off a grey coat, black velvet breeches, with a pair of white trousers over them". In March the same year 1785 Richard Doidge Wadge of Callington advertised that some articles that had been found on a suspicious person at Callington, "(to wit) - four silver tea spoons, marked with the letter S, two I.H; a shirt half made; pillow drawer, marked M.E.C.; great coat, women's and children's stockings, and also a paper purporting to be an agreement, dated February 20, 1785, between Francis Stevens and John Furze, to go to Trinity in Newfoundland, as a salter to Richard Waterman there, two guineas to be paid as an advance when the ship sails over Teignmouth bar. The person on whom the articles were found escaped with his guard at Callington on Sunday night last. He wore away a blue coat, red waistcoat, and nankeen breeches, and has lost the fore finger of his right hand. Whoever has lost any of the above articles, are desired to apply to Mr. Richard Doidge Wadge, in Callington, and they will be informed of particulars."

As Mary Rawling was going home from Camelford to St.Lawrence, near Bodmin on the 22nd of December 1786, she was stopped and robbed of about £2.4s in cash, mercery and grocery goods to the value of about £40 together with the mare the said goods were carried on in hampers, which said mare was an iron grey, about 6 years old, 13 hands and half high, and a meally mouth, by two men, one about 5 feet 7 inches and a half high, the other about 5 feet 6 inches high; who, after they had beat her in a most cruel and barbarous manner, made off with their prize. The robbery was committed about half past nine in the evening, near Mount Charles turnpike gate, nigh the road leading from Wadebridge to Bodmin. Mary Rawling offered ten guineas reward to any person or persons who should apprehend the said men, so as they may be brought to justice.

The same reward was offered in February 1787 for information on the person or persons who did feloniously break open the Cellar Door, belonging to Mr. Niels Falck, merchant, Falmouth, commonly called or known by the name of Treethy's cellar, and broke up two planks of the flooring into the loft, and stole "4 Quoils White rope, 20 small quoils white line, 1 quoil of 21 yards of tarred rope, 1 piece red and 1 piece light blue coarse foreign cloth, 3 pieces linen, 100 yard linen, 8 pieces of sail canvas, 13 yards unbleached, 18 yards of bleached, and 37 yards of striped linen, 43 handkerchiefs, red and white, and blue and white stripes."

A whole lot of silver and plated items were stolen out of the house of Rev. Radcliffe at Stokeclimsland on the night of 24th April 1790, tea kettle, lamp stand, salver, coffee pot, waiters, fish slice, gravy spoon, tea candlestick, sugar tongs, cream ladle, tea spoons, candlesticks, stand for snuffers, tea pot. Rev. Radcliffe offered five guineas for information. Shortly after most of the items were recovered and two men belonging to the company of artillery at Plymouth Dock arrested for the robbery and put in Bodmin gaol. In July a warehouse at Falmouth in which the cargo of the French ship L'Hercule from Port au Prince was deposited was broken into and two bags containing 140 lbs. of raw coffee stolen. The customs commissioners offered £10 for information as did Messrs. Geo. C.Fox, merchants. On 26th November 1791 two silver watches were stolen out of the shop of Benjamin Andrew at St.Austell, one of them marked on the plate, Ransford, London, No.890 and the other Summers, London, No.1945. On 5th December from the same shop went three other watches, one marked Benjamin Andrew

Tehidy Park in Cornwall, the Seat of Sir Francis Bafsett Bar.ᵗ

jun., St.Austell, the second, James Hopwood, No.1787 on the plate and the letters of his name on the dial, with gold hands, and the third, John Neaton, London. Five guineas offered on conviction of the thieves.

PILLS AND MEDICINES

Sickness and illness were other aspects of life that people of the time naturally had to cope with, not so well understood as to-day, of course. Various remedies and treatments were peddled. On account of the great rise in price of Spilsbury's drops which took place on 1st September 1783 Miss Russells at Falmouth laid up a large stock of this celebrated medicine, "so eminently famous for affording speedy relief in cases of the scurvy, gout, rheumatism, nervous complaints &c., prepared by F.Spilsbury, Soho Square, London." The bottles were priced at 4s and 7s each and people were recommended to send in their orders quickly. Mr. Spilsbury's treatise on the scurvy, gout, diet, &c. second edition with the particulars of eighty cures could be lent gratis to read. In 1787 Mrs. Elliot, printer, of Falmouth, had received a supply of Dr.Green's royal antiscorbutic drops, which were famous for curing the scurvy, leprosy, ulcerated legs, the king's evil, cancers, fistulas, piles, rheumatisms, rheumatic gout &c. &c. They were excellent in strengthening the stomach, creating a good appetite and an excellent restorative for decaying constitutions. They could be taken by women with child, young children, and people of the most delicate constitutions. The drops were sold in moulded square bottles at 4s6d the bottle, duty included, with the following inscription blown in the glass, viz. "John Green, only proprietor of the royal antiscorbutic drops". Proofs of their superior efficacy to any medicine hitherto known were published weekly in the paper. "To Mr. Green surgeon, Flushing, near Falmouth, December 23 1786. 'Sir Your absence abroad prevented me from having an opportunity of acknowledging the very extraordinary cure I received by taking your royal antiscorbutic drops. About five years ago I was seized with a violent rheumatism, which deprived me of the use of my limbs. I was seventeen weeks on crutches, dressed and undressed by my wife, for I could not lift my hand to my head: all the doctors who attended me (which were a late doctor of Falmouth, his three sons, and others of the faculty), gave me over, and left me for death; but on hearing on of your bills read, and knowing several of the people who had been cured by your royal antiscorbutic drops, I was determined to make a trial of two bottles, but before I had taken them, I was able to walk with a small stick, and by the time I had finished the sixth bottle I was as well as ever I was in all my life, and have not had the least return of that disorder ever since. I am, sir, your humble servant, William Pearce. P.S. Mr. Elliot, printer of Falmouth, knows me, and will satisfy any one of the truth of the above.' " The drops were sold at Mr.Elliot's and the following places in Cornwall - Mr.Read, Redruth; Mrs. Pawley, Truro; Mr. Hugoe, Penzance; Mr. B.Pascoe, Helston; Mr. Harvey, Penzance; Miss Bond, St.Columb; Mr. Flamank, Bodmin; Mr. J.Pope, Camelford; Mrs. Travossa, Launceston; Mr. T.Hugoe, Penryn. Also at these places could be had Dr.Green's specific drops (without mercury), "so well known to be an absolute cure for every stage of the venereal disease, even if the disorder has been standing twenty years. Price 4s6d the bottle and 6d duty."

More support for Dr.Green's Royal Antiscorbutic drops came in 1790 from a miller at Bessean Mills, St.Just, Oliver Pool, in a similar advertisement. He said "I think it by justice to inform you of the wonderful cure I have received by taking your Royal Antiscorbutic Drops. I was for thirty years dreadfully afflicted with violent pains and sickness in my stomach, attended with frequent dreadful vomitings, and what is called water pangs, to such a degree, that many times I thought I should expire every minute. I had very little appetite and bad digestion. I was greatly oppressed with wind and sour belchings; and from such a complication of disorders I thought myself far advanced in a decline. During my long affliction I applied to the faculty, and was blooded, but it was of no use to me, nor anything else, 'till I took your Royal Antiscorbutic Drops; and what is really astonishing, I got a perfect cure with taking only one small bottle, and have not had the least return these two years".

In 1791 Dr.Thurston's Rheumatic Oil was recommended - "This incomparable oil gives almost instantaneous ease in twenty-four hours of the most violent pains of the Rheumatism and Rheumatic; by a short continuance of its use performs a perfect cure. It is also a most certain remedy for those who have lost the use of their limbs by colds; fevers, bruises, or strains, even if they have been cripples for twenty years. Dr. Thurston strongly recommends his Universal Antiscorbutic Drops to be taken at the time of using the oil, as they will cause a free circulation of the blood, when before in a manner stagnated, and be of the utmost supports to the parts afflicted." The "superior efficacy" of the medicines was shown by "upwards of 1000 persons have already been relieved" including Richard Webber, staymaker of St.Kew, Bodmin who "was for five years violently afflicted with the rheumatism in all his limbs, which rendered him incapable of following his business, being scarce able to dress or undress, even to feed himself for months together, despairing or ever getting relief; but to the astonishment of all his friends he received a perfect cure in a short time by Dr. Thurston's Oil and Drops".

Another remedy that was given support in the pages of the Sherborne Mercury was Dr.Waite's Gingerbread Nuts in 1793. Richard Williams of Redruth sent the maker, J.Evans of 42 Long Lane, West Smithfield, London the testimony of Warren Trestrail who believed "he should have been in the grave before this time, had it not been for Dr.Waite's valuable Worm Nuts". "I, Warren Trestrail, of the parish of Redruth... having for some time been in a bad state of health, I applied to sundry experienced men of the faculty, and they all treated me as in a decline, taking several medicines from them - but of no use - till I was reduced as low that I was not able to walk a hundred yards without stopping to recover my strength and breath; but hearing of Dr.Waite's Gingerbread Nuts, I sent to Redruth to Richard Williams, shopkeeper, for one packet, to try if of any use. I took one in the evening and two in the morning, and soon afterwards I voided one large worm down, and one large worm at my mouth; in two days I was a new man, and by frequent taking of them, I am, by the help of God, restored to my former health and strength; and I find them of so much value, that I keep them in my house for frequent use. Many of my neighbours know this to be true as well as myself".

John Ching of Launceston believed he had a cure for cancers. He had made an improvement on the treatment usually and successfully practised by the late Rev. J. Morgan of Egloskerry. He placed an advertisement in the paper to inform "those whose misfortune has involved them in that dreadful malady, that to him they may apply and assure themselves, that he is possessed of a safe, innocent and effectual cure, by drawing out cancers, root and branch, without the use of the knife, or any other manual instrument, and by administering at the same time, such internal medicines as tend to destroy that humour from which cancers naturally feed; and that all those who are thus afflicted may have an opportunity of experiencing this benefit, the advertiser attends and provides medicines, for those that are really poor, without any other compensation than what results from the pleasure of doing good".

DOCTORS

Doctors could be found in most towns and villages but little reference to their work appeared in the pages of the paper. In April 1788 Dr. Walker put in a notice regarding his taking up the medical practice vacated by Dr.Fox. He "hopes there cannot be any impropriety in returning his sincere thanks to many respectable families, and to the gentlemen of the faculty in Falmouth and the adjacent towns, for the very polite reception and encouragement when offering himself as a Physician to succeed Dr.Fox, on his removal to London. He flatters himself that experience, gained by long and extensive practice, joined to the strictest attention for the recovery or those who please to call for his assistance may, in time, procure him their confidence and approbation. He lodges at Mr. Belthouses, Falmouth".

HOSPITAL

Following a request from several of the principal gentlemen in Cornwall a meeting was held at the Assize Hall, Bodmin on 4th August 1790 to consider the possibility of establishing a county hospital. This clearly won support and a further notice appeared in the paper in September - "As many poor persons are in want of proper care, medicine, and diet, when in sickness, which they cannot receive from their respective parishes, already in many cases overburthened by enormous poor rates, and as many of the said infirm poor are actually lost to the community, and their families, from the circumstances above stated", gentlemen had subscribed to erect a "public infirmary for the sick and lame poor". A list of 17 names was printed headed by Sir John St.Aubyn giving £200 for the building and an annual donation of ten guineas for its maintenance and Sir Francis Basset £200 and an annual 30 guineas. Subsequently the plan for establishing a general infirmary in Cornwall was honoured with the patronage of the Prince of Wales and Duke of Cornwall. Designs for the building were drawn up in 1791 by Mr. Ebdon and in October a meeting of subscribers was held at the Town Hall, Truro to consider tenders for its construction. So were sown the seeds that resulted in the building of the Royal Cornwall Infirmary.

LIBRARY

Around the same time, in 1792, efforts were also made to establish a county library. "At a meeting held this day, for the purpose of taking into a consideration a Plan for establishing a Public County Library, and for illustrating the Antiquities and Natural History of the County of Cornwall, It was resolved, That a subscription be immediately opened for the above purposes, and that no sum less than One Guinea Entrance and One Guinea Annually be received. That a Committee of - persons shall be appointed annually to conduct and manage the purposes of this institution, in the election of whom all subscribers shall have a vote, but no person be chosen of the Committee, who shall subscribe less than two guineas entrance and two guineas annually. that all the Books, Fossils, and other property belonging to this Library shall be vested in the Members of Parliament of the county (being Cornishmen), and in certain public officers of the county, for the time being. That Truro will be the most central and advantageous situation in which to establish such an institution. That a meeting be held at the Metal Company Committee Room, in Truro, on Thursday the 25th day of October next, in order finally to arrange and digest regulations for most effectually carrying into execution the above plan, at which all the subscribers are requested to attend. That subscriptions be received at the Two Banks, in Truro". The following year the treasurer, Francis Enys, put a notice in the paper about holding of a general meeting of subscribers at the Library in Truro at noon on Thursday 29th August. The upshot of these discussions was the establishment of the Royal Institution of Cornwall a few years later in 1818.

BOOKS

There were some references to books in the paper. In November 1783 - "a new Cornwall Almanack will soon be published containing commercial, historical and miscellaneous articles relative to the county. From the diligence and accuracy of the compiler, and the great many articles it comprehends more than can be found in any one publication. It is hoped the public will favour it with their attention". Not long after a lady from Exeter requested that the gentleman to whom her husband, the late Richard Thorn, bookseller, lent Hals's History of Cornwall "will be so obliging to return it... Mr. Thorn's memorandums not having, as yet, discovered to whom it was lent, she hopes the gentleman who has it will excuse this mode of application". In 1790 there was advertised a new book (in fact the second edition) by the Rev. Richard Lyne, master of the free grammar school, Liskeard, "Isagoge, sive Janua Tusculana", an introductory book for grammar schools, and children under private tuition. It was "printed on a fine demy 8vn. price 2s, bound in leather, with blank paper at the end for additional remarks, by the master or scholar". The first part "by means of a few general rules of construction, is calculated to instruct the young scholar, in a very short time, in the act of turning Latin into English, without any assistance from translations, marginal figures, &c." It was on sale at bookshops at Cambridge, Oxford, Eton, Exeter and other parts, in Cornwall at M. Elliott, Falmouth and J.Liddell, Bodmin.

MUSIC AND THE THEATRE

Plays and musical performances were being staged, music being played in the home. Theatres came to be established in Truro and Penzance - one was "new erecting" there in 1786. Letter of September 23, 1789 - "Mr and Mrs. Brown, in their way to the Theatre-Royal, Dublin, have entertained this town [Liskeard] with an histrionic farrago, consisting of a number of petit dramatic pieces, with several comic songs, prologues, &c. which have afforded great satisfaction to the gentlemen and ladies of Liskeard". In 1788 there was offered for sale by Francis Joll of St. Austell "an elegant organ, with a handsome mahogany front, eight feet high, five feet six inches wide, and three feet deep, with seven stops, a stop and open diapason, principal, twelfth, fifteenth, and flute all through, with two short octaves double A & G, a hautboy down to C, with a pedal that takes a st four(?) stops, and leaves the hautboy and both diapasons for the soft organ and swell." On Tuesday 23rd July 1793 at 10 a.m. in Madron church there was "a sacred concert of vocal and instrumental music, in three parts, selected from Handel's Oratorio, the Messiah. Part I. Overture, Messiah. Air, 'Comfort ye my people, &c.' Air, 'Ev'ry valley &c.' Overture, Jomellis Air 'He shall seed his stock, &c.' Overture Richard 1st. Part II. Overture, Esther. Air, 'The trumpet shall sound &c.' The 100th Psalm paraphrased. Air, 'I know that my Redeemer liveth, &c.' Overture, Berenice, Part III. Overture, Saul, with the Dead March. Air, 'Our Lord is risen from the Dead, &c' Sixth Concerto Gemaniani, (Opera Quarta.) Occasional Oratorio. To conclude with the Grand Chorus, Hallelujah. Tickets were obtainable from Mr. Commins, Mr. Holkleg, churchwarden, Mr. Hewett, stationer and Mr. Fleming at the Post Office, at 2s6d each." Profits were applied to charitable purposes for the poor of Madron and Penzance not receiving parish pay. No person "could possibly be admitted without a ticket".

CLUBS

Inns and some coffee houses provided social centres in towns and villages. Clubs were also being established. In 1787 the Oxford Cornish Club held its anniversary at the Red Lion, Truro on Wednesday 29th July. Dinner on the table at 4 p.m. Later in the year the Penzance Card Assembly announced that it would commence at the Ship and Castle Inn on Tuesday 11th September and "be continued every Tuesday fortnight the season". In 1789 was established "a Club for supporting the independency of the county, the gentlemen, clergy, and freeholders, are hereby informed, that the first meeting of the club will be at the King's Head, Truro on Monday the 12th October 1789. The club will be held alternately in the towns of Truro, Launceston, Bodmin and Helston, every three months. The club is open to all freeholders... Dinner on the table at two o'clock precisely, Sir William Molesworth, Bart. in the chair. Ordinary one shilling". Further meetings were held at Launceston on 12th January 1790, with William Symons Esq., in the chair, in the same town on 26th July 1792 with Colonel Morshead, at Truro on 20th September 1793 Sir William Molesworth. Other meetings were no doubt held. Molesworth was also behind the formation of the Cornwall Agricultural Society at a meeting at Bodmin on 1st December 1792, this initiating the subsequent Royal Cornwall Shows.

SPORTS

Various other leisure and sporting activities were advertised. On 9th June 1783 at the house of William Fry, the Rose and Crown, Millbrook there was a wrestling match, the prize a gold-laced waistcoat. Each man to throw two men a fair fall on the back, and to be eight standers, and not to play after nine o'clock at night. On the following day a silver cup to be wrestled for on the same conditions, the winner of each prize having to spend five shillings each at the same house. The man that won the prize on the first day was not allowed to play the second day. On Wednesday 11th a silver laced hat was cudgelled for and there were to be eight standers. Each man that broke two fair heads became a stander. The man that won the prize had to spend two shillings and sixpence. As well there was jack ass racing, the prize a silver horse.

There was wrestling and cudgelling at games at Maker Green, near Kingsand and Cawsand on Wednesday 23rd June 1784 and the following two days. The prizes on the first day an handsome silver cup, three guineas value, for the first best man; a gold lace hat, one guinea value, for the second; and half-a-guinea for the third. The second day, a large elegant silver bowl, six guineas value, for the first best man; two guineas for the second; and one guinea for the third. The third day, a gold lace hat, one guinea value, will also be wrestled for. Each day there was also running for pigs, racing by asses, running for smocks and jumping in bags, with several other kinds of diversions. In the advertisement it was said "Every civility and kind attention will be paid to the spectators. The games to begin each day at ten a.m." Similar games were advertised in June 1785 with the addition of bull-baiting on two days, the best dog receiving a silver collar of one guinea value and five shillings for the second best dog. There was wrestling on Cokesland Common, near Bodmin, on Thursday 26th October 1786. Five guineas to the winner, three to the second, two to the third best wrestlers. Many gentlemen were said to be attending and great encouragement given to the wrestlers.

In 1791 Liskeard's Annual Diversions were held on the Monday and Tuesday in Whitsun week. The best man in cudgelling received four guineas, second best one guinea, standers 2/6 on the first day; on the second first one guinea, second half a guinea and standers 2/6. The best man in the wrestling on the first day received one guinea, second half a guinea and standers shilling; on the second day, first four guineas, second one guinea and standers 2/6. It was said that "strangers will receive every encouragement. Conditions to be seen at the field". There was wrestling at St. Columb Major on Monday 5th September. The best man had a purse of guineas, the second best two guineas, and the third a gold-laced hat. "Three impartial sticklers will be appointed, and be on the ground precisely at one o'clock in the afternoon, at which time the wrestling will begin. Great encouragement will be given to all good players, and every step taken to preserve the greatest order and fair play". The following year the wrestling was held on Monday 18th June, the only difference in the prizes being that the best man received an "handsome piece of plate". At Helston there was wrestling on Helston Down on Tuesday 24th September, starting at 10 a.m. "The rules will be then fixed, and every man may depend on fair play". The first prize was six guineas, the second three and the third one.

Horse races were held on Bodmin Down on Tuesday 21st of September 1784. The principal prize was a silver bowl, value £50 given by the members for the county, for the winner of three heats over the four miles course. On the 22nd the prize was a plate of £50, given by the Members for Bodmin, and a similar prize the following day for horses that had never won £50 at a time. Horses were handicapped by age and weight. Non-subscribers paid two guineas entrance, or double at the post; subscribers or givers of any or either of the plates half. The horses running for each of the above plates had to be entered with the clerk of the course at the White Hart Inn, Bodmin on Friday the 17th September, between the hours of two and five in the afternoon. Races started at noon and none but subscribers of half a guinea were allowed to erect booths. Similar races were held in 1786 and 1787 with similar conditions and prizes. In 1786 it was added that "all disputes arising on the course to be determined by the majority of the subscribers to the free plate present. Assemblies and ordinaries for the ladies and gentlemen as usual. Stewards - Colonel Boscawen and Weston Helyar Esq." In 1787 the stewards were Humphrey Prideaux Esq. and J.P.Foote, Esq.

Borlase referred to the holding of cock fighting matches. A notice of "Cocking" was put in the paper by "Feeders", Watling and Burtt in 1792. "A main of cocks to be fought, at Launceston, in the county of Cornwall, between the Gentlemen of Cornwall and the Gentlemen of Dorset; to shew 41 cocks on each side; to weigh Monday the 4th of June, and fight the three following days, for 10 guineas each battle, and 200 guineas the main".

Hunting was a great sport of the time though not greatly referred to in the paper. There were a couple of advertisements for helpers. In 1782 - "Wanted immediately, a stout active young man, that understands something of hare-hunting. No one need apply unless he can produce a good character to Mr. Wood, innkeeper,

Pengersick Castle, Cornwall.

Western Taphouse, 22nd September". In the late 80s - "Wanted for a gentlemen in Cornwall, a good groom, who also understands somewhat of hunting and to take care of a few harriers, and to wait at table occasionally. N.B. None need apply but those who can have an undeniable good character from his last place. Enquire of the printers of this paper, or of Mr. Norway, at Lostwithiel."

FAIRS

Fairs afforded periodic entertainment. Whereas St.Luke's Fair, usually held on the 29th and 30th October, at the village of St.Lawrence, in the parish of Bodmin, and the 29th October in 1785 being on a Saturday, the fair was held on Monday and Tuesday 31st October and 1st November. The amendment advertised by Thomas Hicks and William Stephens, farmers of the fair. It being understood that a general thanksgiving for the restoration of his Majesty's health was to be appointed to be held on the 23rd April 1789, arrangements were made to hold Menheniot fair the following day but should the thanksgiving be at another time the fair would be held as normal. The same year Saltash fair, usually held within the borough of Saltash on St.James's day, was postponed until Wednesday the 29th July 1789. There were to be "the usual diversions".

In September 1790 it was announced a Show of Cattle was to be held at Ponsanooth in the parish of St.Gluvias, near Penryn on St. Matthew's day the 21st. Another show would be held on the Tuesday following the first Sunday in May following, to be continued annually on these dates. "Whoever is pleased to support it with their interest by bringing their cattle, &c. may depend on the greatest encouragement possible. Proper standings will be erected, and due attendance given." Shortly after it was announced that Matthew's fair at Liskeard which was usually held on the 2nd October, since that year it fell on a Saturday would be held on the following Monday, the 4th. In 1792 a similar notice about the change of date concerned the fair held at Trevena, Tintagel. Usually it was held on the 19th, that year it would be held on Monday the 22nd October.

A tragic accident occurred at Redruth fair on 12th October 1791. "Two horses on full gallop, having set off in contrary directions, unfortunately met head to head, with such violence, that both horses and one of the riders (a young man about 17 years of age) were killed on the spot. The other rider is so shockingly maimed as to render his recovery doubtful".

CELEBRATIONS

Celebrations on the occasion of notable events and other festivities were periodically held. "Extract of a letter from Saltash, September 26 1787. Yesterday a ball was given by Major Lemon, Member of this town, to the ladies and gentlemen of the neighbourhood. Saltash and its vicinity have long been celebrated for pretty women; and never was a brighter blaze of beauty displayed in any assembly than on the present occasion. The room was decorated with his Majesty's arms, and other insignia expressive of that loyalty, which the worthy member has from principle always testified towards his sovereign. The company began to assemble about 8 o'clock, and before 9 the new assembly room of 80 feet long, which was fitted up for the purpose, was so filled that there was scarce room for the dancers. Several persons of the first distinction were present, whose affability did honour to their rank, and encreased the general satisfaction felt on an occasion so interesting to all true friends to the freedom of election. About 12 o'clock a most elegant supper was served, after which a number of loyal and constitutional toasts were drunk. His Majesty's health was accompanied with 21 cheers, the Duke of Cornwall with three times three, which was followed by those of Mr. Lemon and the freeholders, Sir Wm. Lemon, his brother, the worthy representatives of the county, Mr. Buller of Morval, and others who had exerted themselves in restoring the antient rights of the borough. The respectable appearance made on this occasion plainly evinces that the cause and the supporters of it have met with the universal approbation of the country. The festivity was by no means confined to the hall room; it was diffused through the whole town, and long will the worthy freeholders of Saltash remember the very handsome manner in which their truly respectable and independent members shewed his gratitude for their distinguished favours. About 2 o'clock the dancing recommended, which was kept up with great spirit till daylight. The general cheering in the streets and publick houses, the ringing of bells, and the firing of cannon from the yachts in the river, exhibited a scene of universal joy and satisfaction."

On 23rd March 1789 at St. Ives - "The manner in which this borough was illuminated last night on account of his Majesty's happy recovery, exceeded all of the kind ever remembered in this neighbourhood. It is impossible to describe what a profusion of joy was manifested by the inhabitants at large; each strove to outvie each other in splendor on this happy occasion. Hugh Giddy Esq. distributer of the stamps, took upon himself the management, and gave orders to the constables, beadles &c. to parade the streets, by which means the greatest good order was preserved. The house of the late Mr. Richard Dotty had a most splendid appearance; the lamps were variegated and hung in festoons, and in the middle window of the second story there appeared a beautiful transparent painting of the King's head, and over it 'Long live the King'. James Polkinghorne, Esq. had a lamp hung before every pane of glass in his house. The rooms were also superbly lighted within. About eight o'clock at night he was borne on the shoulders of six Captains of Ding Dong Tin Mine (in which he is principally concerned) in a kebbel, elegantly decorated with variegated lamps; a young lady dressed as Britannia carried a transparent canopy over his head, with a green inscription, 'May the King live forever'. On his return to his house he was received by three huzzas, and a display of above 300 sky and wheel rockets. It is worthy of remark that five foreign Captains, who put into this port during the winter in distress, decorated their vessels in a very elegant manner, and all heartily joined the loyal gentlemen's party at the Red Lion".

A letter from Marazion on 21st June 1791 - "Last Saturday the Duke and Duchess of Leeds arrived at Godolphin House, near this town, the seat of the late Lord Godolphin, but now belonging to the Duke. Godolphin, formerly Godolgan, which, according to some, signifies in the Cornish-Belgic a Wood Down, has been the seat of the Godolphin family since the reign of Henry VII, when that monarch changed the name of Godolphin, alleging that 'as his virtues had given him the title of Pater patrie, he should be called after the name of that place of which he was Lord'. The arrival of his Grace was announced by bonfires on the hills, firing of cannons, ringing of bells in all the neighbouring parishes, and such other demonstrations of joy as were never seen by the oldest inhabitants of Cornwall. But though these were all the tokens of respect which gratitude could give, yet they fainly express the obligations which the Cornish owe to this illustrious visiter. In the late and present distress of the miners his Grace has adventured largely in the mines, entirely with the benevolent design of keeping the poor employed; and in order to invite others to cooperate with him, he generously gave up the tin-dues, to which, as lord of the soil, he is entitled. It is much to be wished that his Grace's conduct in this respect may be followed by all the land holders in this county, though it is certainly without precedent. The great affability and condescension of the Duke, as well as of the amiable Dutchess, and her sister, even to the lowest members of society, are at present much admired, and will be long remembered. It is said his Grace intends visiting the Scilly Islands".

Plans were made to erect the "much-wished for Quay at Trevaunance Porth" in the summer of 1792. Designed by an eminent architect of London, Richard Wooding, it was to be erected with all possible expedition. "The parish [of St.Agnes] and indeed the northern part of the county (to say nothing of the number of lives which most likely will be saved from the asylum it will afford to vessels in distress), will reap considerable advantages from it. The scheme of the Quay was first projected by that tried friend of the tinners, Mr. Oates, a native of St.Agnes, but now a considerable merchant of Penryn, in honour to whom the innocent sports of the country, such as wrestling, football, &c. were on the 31st ult. [August] practised with infinite hilarity and good humour; and at night there was a grand illumination at the church tower, and bonfires on the surroundings hills; although some thousand persons were assembled, not a single accident happened to break in upon the festivity of the day. The tinners' friend was attended by Messrs. Biky and Hoblyn, of London, Prout, Tregellas, and others, the principal gentlemen of the parish".

NEWS ITEMS: TRAGEDIES AND ESCAPES

As well as advertisements and public and legal notices there was a column, which became more detailed in later issues, giving reports of news of interest, accidents, deaths, weather details etc. Tragic accidents - a letter from Mevagissey, October 17, 1786 "last Sunday as William Harris and Richard Tallack were on the cliffs at Pentowan, about two miles from this place, they saw a piece of timber in the sea, in attempting to secure which the waves drew Harris off, and he was unfortunately drowned. Tallack saved himself by laying hold of the rocks. Harris's body is not yet found." A letter from Tregony on Christmas day 1789 - "A melancholy accident happened here on Sunday morning. Mrs. Middlecoat, at the Queen's Head Inn, left her child, a boy, about three weeks old, in a half tester turn-up bed. Some time after she sent up a maid servant to see if he was quiet, who returned saying that he was sleeping very sweet; about 15 or 20 minutes later, the same servant having occasion for some raisins which were in a cupboard by the side of the bed, through a strange unaccountable and fatal absence of mind, hastily turned up the bed, and left it so, by which means the poor infant was smothered. The distress of the unhappy mother (who herself found her child in the situation before mentioned), and , in short, of the whole family is indescribable. every means that the faculty could devise were tried, but, alas! without effect. The servant, the innocent cause (unintentionally) of this scene of woe, has continued in a very distracted state ever since. It has been remarked, that she has always conducted herself in a very affectionate manner to the children of the family".

In March 1790 - "Some days since a vessel was entirely lost on the Runnel Stone, near Land's End, but the crew are saved; the next day three young men venturing to go out on a rock, to get near the wreck, a wave washed them off, and they were all drowned. Two of the bodies are since found, one of them was without a head". In May 1791 - "Thursday se'nnight a melancholy accident happened near St.Ives: A fishing boat reaching towards shore, was overtaken by a sudden gust of wind, which threw her on her side, and she immediately foundered. Out of four men therein one only was saved". July 1791 - "Sunday se'nnight, in the evening about ten o'clock, the following melancholy accident happened at Restronget Passage, near Truro. A small passage boat having taken several passengers and three horses on board, when, about half way over, one of the horses took fright, and in attempting to leap into the water overturned the boat, when three of the passengers, viz, a Miss Fellowe, of Penryn, - from Birmingham, and one of the boatmen were unfortunately drowned. This should caution boatmen against the imprudence of over crowding their boats, a practice too frequent in Cornwall".

In a letter from Mevagissey on 24th January 1792 - "Saturday last a shocking accident happened at Polgooth tin mine, in the parish of St.Mewan. A child, four years ago, son of Thomas May, one of the miners, fell into a shaft about eight fathom deep; the mother after searching for the child, heard its cries at the bottom, and went and called for assistance. The father and others came and called to the child, who answered that he was not hurt but only wet. But in lowering a man down, a stone fell from the top on the child's head, which fractured its skull in such a manner, that it expired a few minutes after it was brought to the top of the pit". Late February 1792 - "Thursday se'nnight as Mr. John Bone, shoemaker, of Fowey, was going over Lostwithiel bridge, he fell into the river, and was drowned". May 1792 - "On the 15th instant, a melancholy accident happened at Padstow: several children were at play on a large piece of mahogany then lying on the quay, the ground on which it stood suddenly gave way, and the piece of mahogany fell on one of the children (a fine boy about six years old), and struck his head in so terrible a manner that he expired instantly". Writing from Fowey on 20th June 1792 - "Saturday last a child belonging to Mr. John Hole, mason, of Lanteglos, near this town, fell into the river, and was unfortunately drowned".

In the autumn of 1792 - "Tuesday John Long, senior, a blacksmith, of St.Austell, and who farmed the markets of that town, hung himself in his own chamber. the immediate cause of this rash act is supposed to be a quarrel he had the day before, when intoxicated, with his wife and friends. The same day one John Stiles, an old man in the workhouse of St.Austell, also hung himself. And a man who lived in Gorran, a parish near St.Austell, also hung himself. The cause is unknown".

The occasional miraculous escape. June 1791 - "One day last week a child 17 months old fell into a tin pit, 48 yards deep, in the parish of Germo... and only received a slight wound over the eye. This is more surprizing as the bottom of the pit was covered with large rocks".

FIRES

Fires were also reported. July 1792 - "On the morning of the 18th ult. the Rev. Mr. Honey's house, at Trenant, in the parish of Menheniot... was set on fire by the carelessness of two maid servants, and entirely consumed. They had made a fire under a furnace, for the purpose of washing, and leaving it in order to drink tea, it communicated to some fuel that lay near, and from thence to the floor of the rooms where the men servants and boys were sleeping. By this accident Mr. Honey, and his tenant, Mr. John Snell, will sustain a loss of more than £2000".

UNUSUAL CRIMES

And unusual or remarkable crimes. In August 1792 - "Last week some boys, as they were playing on the common between Helston and Marazion, by accident took up a turf, and under it discovered the funnel of a chimney under the surface of the earth. On looking down they saw a grate with cinders in it, which exciting their curiosity they went down into a tin-pit not far distant, from whence they found a passage into this subterranean house, which appeared to be a coiner's shop. Here they found almost all the apparatus used in coining money, especially crowns, half-crowns, and shillings, for which there were molds, together with several pieces of pewter-dishes, and base metal, being a mixture of silver and pewter. The pick-axe and shovel, with which the house had been dug, were likewise found there, and many other things. Notice of this discovery was given to a neighbouring magistrate, who issued a warrant, and directed the constables to watch at night, but by this time the matter was become too public to expect to apprehend the delinquents".

"At Summer Court Fair [1793], near Michell... held annually on Holy Thursday, a gang of sharpers under the guise of pedlars, consisting of upwards of 30 persons, men and women, found means to pick the pockets of about half-a-dozen men in the course of the day, to the amount of four score guineas and upwards. They went from thence to Penryn fair, held the 13th instant, where it is much to be hoped a number of them will be detected."

DEATHS

Deaths of notable citizens. In October 1790 - "On Wednesday the 13th instant died, and on Friday last was buried, aged 69 years, Capt. George Oake, late of this place, and formerly commander of a packet boat in the service of the General Post Office. All who had the pleasure of knowing this good man cannot fail to regret his loss, and those who had not that pleasure are hereby truly informed that he possessed every moral, social, and manly virtue; and that during his whole life, which he passed through with unsullied reputation, he was distinguished by tokens of sincere veneration, and that he died lamented, as he had lived respected and esteemed". July 1791 - "A few days since at Penryn, much regretted, Mrs. Rosewarne, the widow of Henry Rosewarne, Esq. deceased, late Vicewarden of the Stannaries of Cornwall, and Member of Parliament for Truro." Writing from Fowey on 20th June 1792 - "Wednesday died Lieutenant Arthur of the Royal Navy, after a few days illness".

In the autumn of 1792 - "Last week died William Tonkin, many years chief bailiff of the stanneries of Cornwall. His death, which happened at Truro, having been unhappily occasioned by his falling through a hole in one of the decayed bridges there into the mud, which is supposed to have stifled him; it is seriously hoped, that this accident, after the other fatal instances that recently occurred of the necessity of speedily repairing them, will properly operate on the Corporation, or those whose duty it is to be at that trifling expence, without which many valuable lives will continue in imminent danger." In March 1793 - "Thursday died, at his appartments in Exeter, after one day's illness, - Lyne, Esq., son of Rev. Dr. Lyne, of Mevagissey, Cornwall. He had been for some short time in that city raising an independent company for the service of Government, and had just completed it, when he was taken ill, which deprived him of life, as well as the enjoyment of his patriotic exertion."

"On Thursday the 25th day of April last [1793] died at Penzance, Richard Oxnam, Esq. in the 63rd year of his age; an eminent and respectable merchant. His loss will be severely felt by all who knew him, for his life was one continued System of public utility and benevolence. His domestic character was above praise - and his family lament, with the sincerest grief and affection, a kind and indulgent parent. His charitable disposition is fully evinced in the handsome legacies bequeathed by him for ever to the poor, not receiving pay, of various parishes, amounting in the whole to no less a sum than £1000 in different annuities. But what above all distinguished his unblemished name, was his meekness and affability, ready at all times to listen to the complaints of the oppressed, and to relieve their wants. He died in the full assurance of immortal life, conscious of being admitted into that happy place, where the righteous receive the reward of their deeds." In September 1793 - "A few days since died at Helston... Mr. Joseph Michell, attorney at law, of that place, after a long and severe fit of the palsy".

MARRIAGES

In early 1790 - "Tuesday last was married at Verian, in Cornwall, Mr. T.Williams, tinman and brazier, of Truro, to Miss Colger; a young lady whose qualifications do honour to her sex, and possessed of a genteel fortune, the reward of industry and merit". June 1791 - "Lately was married at Helston... John Stephens Esq. Penpraze, in the parish of Sithney, to Miss Mary Thomas, daughter of the late Richard Thomas, Esq., an agreeable young lady, with a fortune of £20,000". August 22nd 1791 - "Wednesday last was married, Mr. John Gedye of New Hall, in St.Neot... to Miss Dangger of the same place; a young lady with a handsome fortune, and every other accomplishment to make the marriage state happy". "On the same day a very extraordinary circumstance took place at the parish of Lansallos, near Fowey... About nine years back a young man (a fisherman) courted a young woman of the same place, and proposed to marry her; her father seemed much irritated at the proposal, and declared it never should take place; immediately after the girl took to her bed, declaring she would never more eat bread; she continued in her bed and room for upwards of five years, at the end of which time her father was prevailed upon to admit the young man to visit her; the young man readily accepted the offer, and has continued so to do as often as opportunities would admit; But she had not been known to have been out of her bed more than once for these last four years, nor to have eaten bread or bread-kind ever since she first took to her bed; but to the great surprize and satisfaction of all her friends, she last Tuesday got out of bed, and came down stairs, and the next morning the young couple were married in the presence of a large number of spectators".

BIRTHS

In November 1790 - "Tuesday the lady of Joseph Beauchamp, esq. of Pengreep in Gwennap, near Truro, was brought to bed of a son and heir to that ancient family. The bells in the neighbourhood were rung on the occasion, and other marks of joy were shewn".

METEOR AND EARTHQUAKE

Unusual celestial and planetary manifestations. In May 1790 "A meteor, in magnitude apparently equal to the moon, was seen at Penzance on Tuesday se'nnight,

St Michael's Mount, Cornwall, Plz.

about 11 o'clock at night. It was discovered in the zenith, moving in a southerly direction with wonderful rapidity, and continued visible for the short space of 10 or 12 seconds only, gradually diminishing in size previous to its disappearance. Such was the brilliancy of this meteor, that though there was no moonlight at the time, it illuminated the heavens nearly as much as the sun at noon-day". In a letter from Probus on 18th January 1792 - "Last Sunday about four o'clock in the morning, the shock of an earthquake was felt here, and about the same time in the parish of St.Clements, about three miles hence; it is therefore supposed to have taken a north-east direction; the shock was instantaneous, not continuing a second time, but very perceptible".

ANTI-SLAVERY

The anti-slavery movement was growing in strength and in 1791 a petition was drawn up at Truro to parliament for the abolition of the slave trade, this following a meeting of the mayor, aldermen, capital burgesses and inhabitants of the borough. "That your petitioners cannot, without increasing horror, behold the continuance of a traffick, by which great numbers of human beings are undeservedly dragged from their native home, and consigned to a state that, however modified, is in itself the lowest gradation of human misery... the system of slavery strikes the common sense of mankind as unjust, by observing that all arguments in its favour are drawn from political expedience... neither the real prosperity of individuals, nor any part of the glory of the British empire, can possibly rest on the foundation of crimes that call aloud for the vengeance of Heaven." They called for "the total Abolition of the African Slave Trade... which reflects disgrace on a nation professing principles of civil liberty".

LOYAL ADDRESSES

Following the proclamation of the king against sedition etc. in 1792 loyal addresses were sent by some local boroughs. Writing from Fowey on 20th June 1792 - "Saturday last, pursuant to notice, the Mayor, Aldermen, and inhabitants, met for the purpose of addressing his Majesty on the late proclamation, when a most loyal address was voted unanimously, and ordered to be sent to Lord Valletort, (one of our members) to be presented by him to his Majesty". At a meeting held at Truro on 10th July an address was unanimously approved. "We your Majesty's dutiful and loyal subjects, assembled at a general meeting in the borough of Truro, pursuant to public notice, unite in offering to your Majesty our sincere thanks for your paternal attention to your subjects in issuing your late Proclamation, guarding them against seditious writings, published and industriously circulated for the purpose of exciting groundless discontents and jealousies in the minds of your Majesty's loyal subjects respecting the laws and constitution of this kingdom. We beg leave to assure your Majesty of our detestation of such proceedings, and our abhorrence of such correspondences with persons in foreign parts, which aim at the subversion of all regular government, and are inconsistent with the peace and good order of society. And we further assure your Majesty of our zealous attachment to the present form of our constitution, to which under Divine Favour, we are indebted for our unexampled happiness and prosperity; and that we will avoid, and, to the utmost of our power, discourage and prevent all proceedings tending to promote riots and tumults; and that we will in every mode, warranted by law, cordially join in discovering the authors and publishers of all measures tending to interrupt the public peace and tranquillity". A copy of the address was sent to all market towns in the county for signature, for fourteen days from the 26th July, and was inserted twice in the Sherborne Mercury. The sheriff was requested to inform the constables of the several hundreds details of the proceedings of the meeting.

On 31st December 1792, a group in Fowey produced another - "We the undersigned (formerly, with others, constituting a club by the name of the Fishing Club), from the present situation of public affairs, did request that the Mayor of this borough would be pleased to convene a Meeting of the Inhabitants, that we might have an opportunity of publicly testifying our attachment to our beloved Sovereign, and our present happy constitution; but no attention having been paid to our request, we find it incumbent on us, being truly sensible of the many advantages which we and our fellow subjects enjoy under our present happy constitution, and being actuated by a steady and affectionate loyalty to the best of Kings, to solemnly declare, That we will, in our several stations, behave in a peaceable and orderly manner, as becomes faithful, loyal, and good subjects to our King and the established laws of our country. That we will do all in our power to aid and assist the magistracy in maintaining the general tranquillity, in suppressing all riots and disturbances, and in bringing the authors and promoters thereof to condign punishment." They were nervous times with the French revolution followed by war with that country and economic problems at home and riots by tinners and others. The nine signatories resolved to publish their address in the Sherborne Mercury and other papers and copies were put up in conspicuous places in the borough. At a meeting at Bodmin on 4th March 1793 organised by the sheriff, Francis Glanville, consideration was given to the late riots in Cornwall and what measures needed to be taken to prevent their repetition. The riots were condemned and the punishment of the leaders urged. Corn should be transported by sea. The clerk of the peace to receive information about the rioters. Thanks were given to Lieut-Gov. Campbell for his readiness in rendering military assistance. The resolutions were published in the Sherborne Mercury and distributed throughout Cornwall.